# Japan's Road to Pluralism

The Japan Center for International Exchange wishes to thank

**The Nippon Foundation**

# Japan's
# Road to Pluralism

## Transforming Local Communities in the Global Era

*edited by*
Furukawa Shun'ichi
*and*
Menju Toshihiro

Japan Center for International Exchange • *Tokyo* • *New York*

The surnames of the authors and other persons mentioned in this book are positioned according to country practice.

Copyediting by Pamela J. Noda and Lidia Rényi
Cover and typographic design by Becky Davis, EDS Inc., Editorial & Design Services. Typesetting and production by EDS Inc.
Cover photograph © 1999 Jeremy Woodhouse/PhotoDisc, Inc.

Printed in Japan
ISBN 4-88907-060-5

Distributed outside Japan by Brookings Institution Press (1775 Massachusetts Avenue, N.W., Washington, D.C. 20036-2188 U.S.A.) and Kinokuniya Company Ltd. (5-38-1 Sakuragaoka, Setagaya-ku, Tokyo 156-8691 Japan).

Japan Center for International Exchange
9-17 Minami Azabu 4-chome, Minato-ku, Tokyo 106-0047 Japan
URL: http://www.jcie.or.jp

Japan Center for International Exchange, Inc. (JCIE/USA)
274 Madison Avenue, Suite 1102, New York, N.Y. 10016 U.S.A
URL: http://www.jcie.org

# Contents

# Foreword

Today, Japan is moving toward becoming a more pluralistic society, and transformation at the local level is particularly evident. Local governments are confronting many new challenges of governance, such as how to overcome the tight fiscal situation, how to formulate policies related to foreign residents that integrate them into society, and how to interact with a newly vocal civil society in the form of nonprofit organizations. The transformation toward pluralism is pervading political, administrative, societal, and business arenas where dominant actors are no longer present.

This volume is the product of a project held under the Global ThinkNet and CivilNet clusters of activities of the Japan Center for International Exchange (JCIE). These two clusters aim to promote, respectively, international networks of policy research institutions and individuals, and collaborative networks of civil society organizations and individuals. The project—"Transformation of Japanese Communities and the Emerging Local Agenda"—studied the impact of globalization on local governance. Under the guidance of Furukawa Shun'ichi, professor of policy and planning sciences at the University of Tsukuba, and Menju Toshihiro, senior program officer of JCIE, five young Japanese scholars and think tank researchers spent a year working toward completion of their papers through attending seminars and workshops and making research trips.

From March 13 to 22, 2001, the study group held a workshop and study tour in San Francisco under the auspices of the Public Policy Institute of California (PPIC). Workshop discussions focused on globalization and the local government, and were based on presentations given by both Japanese participants and the PPIC researchers. The Japanese participants visited Silicon Valley to study the activities of nonprofit organizations and local government and had a series of meetings with the Silicon Valley Network, the San Mateo County Government, and others.

I would like to express sincere gratitude to the authors who participated in this project for the serious effort that they put into their analyses and for contributing their expertise. Special thanks are due to Furukawa Shun'ichi and Menju Toshihiro for their insightful leadership throughout the project. The project and this publication would not have been possible without the generous financial support provided by the Nippon Foundation, to which JCIE extends its special thanks. I would also like to recognize the invaluable assistance of JCIE staff who worked on this project at different phases, especially Hayashi Rika, program associate. Finally, I wish to thank Pamela J. Noda and Kawaguchi Chie of JCIE for their tireless efforts to ensure that this publication came to fruition.

Yamamoto Tadashi
PRESIDENT
JAPAN CENTER FOR INTERNATIONAL EXCHANGE

# Introduction: The Challenges Facing Japanese Communities

## Furukawa Shun'ichi

Disparate changes are occurring and transforming the once stable but static Japanese society. Quite a few journalists and scholars, including sociologists and economists, have unsatisfactorily provided accounts of causes and consequences of these changes. Conceivable causes are not limited to societal and demographic changes, but related to more fundamental value systems and institutions that underlie the foundation of society. And the consequences are not an extension of the past.

At the outset of the new century, Japan is moving toward becoming a more pluralistic society on a par with other societies. Japanese society is often described as a paternalistic type of society where government and business play a dominant role in a congenial relationship, and civil society is comparatively weak, if not nonexistent (Wolferen 1989; Johnson 1995). However, this contention is not free from challenges. While the institutional setting is different, pluralistic transformation is in progress. This transformation is pervading political, administrative, societal, and business arenas where dominant actors are no longer present.

The chapters in this volume address some of the major metamorphoses Japan shall experience and the challenges it faces in the first decade of the twenty-first century. By focusing on the framework and implications of the anticipated transformations, including decentralization schemes and public finance policies, emerging nonprofit organizations (NPOs) and community businesses, multi-ethnic communities, as well as international policies and think tanks, the authors have outlined the changing nature of communities in Japan, and the degree to which this advanced capitalist society is rapidly becoming a mature but ailing welfare state.

The purpose of this book is to provide an overview of Japan's current position, what it wishes to achieve, how this might best be attained, and what challenges it faces. To this end, the focus has been placed on two basic and related concepts, namely, governance and institutions.

## GOVERNANCE

In considering the implications of governance in present-day Japan, the place of such concepts as shared power and civil society must be borne in mind. Advanced countries have seen significant developments in the area of governance during the past few decades, with the "retreat of the State" (Strange 1996), or the erosion of traditional political power. The institutional strength of the nation-state has been limited by a number of factors. First, international compacts and institutions have undermined the sovereign power of nations, as a result of which few countries have been able to make independent decisions, supranational institutions and organizations having become major partners even in domestic policymaking. Second, the nation-state has been challenged in its bid to render services to citizens, deregulation and privatization being perceived as able to provide a solution to the deficits and inadequate public policies that plague the modern welfare state.

Rhodes defines governance based on the British experience in the 1980s and 1990s, describing it as "a new process of governing; or a changed condition of ordered rule; or the new method by which society is governed" (1997, 46). He concentrates on coordination in society as manifest in different types of networks and partnerships. The concept of governance is also being applied to the private sector: Corporate governance is the management system that allows the optimum relationship to be realized among corporate stakeholders, namely, shareholders, customers, suppliers, and communities. In most public and political debate, the term governance is used with reference to sustaining coordination and coherence among a wide variety of actors each with their own respective objectives, such as political actors and institutions, corporate interests, civil society, and transnational organizations (Pierre 2000, 3–4).

The concept of shared power originally referred to the separation of powers in government as is found in many constitutional systems. It has come to include territorial power sharing, typical of the federal system, and partnerships in which private or nonprofit actors share the stakes involved in delivering services to the public (Kettle 1993).

The concept of civil society, meanwhile, refers to the decentralization of governmental power and broader citizen participation in domestic and external policy–related issues. The present-day model is not the same as that which the nineteenth-century German philosopher Georg Wilhelm Friedrich Hegel defined and criticized as being a system of individual self-seeking but, rather, the uncoerced area of human association in which individuals volunteer their resources to achieve a vision of a better community or society. The model encompasses the concept of philanthropy. The term civil society was common in European political thought in the seventeenth and eighteenth centuries in Britain, Holland, France, and the North American colonies. The rise of a capitalist class, the ideology of the separation of the state from society, and insistence on the legitimacy of nonstate organizations in the conduct of public affairs all contributed to the development of this concept.

The recent emergence of civil society organizations in many countries is the result of an attempt to overcome the malfunctioning of states during the twentieth century. And while there may not yet be an "associational revolution" (Salamon and Anheier 1996) in Japan, significant changes are, nevertheless, occurring (Yamamoto 1995; Yamamoto 1998). Japan's central and local governments are often described as traditionally paying more attention to citizens with vested interests than to vesting attention in citizens' interests. Be that as it may, many citizens have, in recent years, begun participating in voluntary community activities, including environmental protection and the aiding of disaster victims, and their power has expanded greatly. Also emerging has been the tendency for citizens to be more sensitive to the wasting of taxpayers' money: The election of reformist candidates in traditionally conservative prefectures in three recent gubernatorial elections reflects the growing popular concern with financial misdemeanors.

In summarizing the concept of governance, four models by Janet Newman (2001) are worth considering. Her two-dimensional configuration shows the degree of centralization or decentralization, as well as the orientation of change.

1. The hierarchical model, oriented toward centralization, continuity, and control, in which the state exerts direct control and change is slow.

2. The rational goal model, with a shorter-range focus oriented toward maximizing output, in which power is dispersed although control is mainly centralized.

3. The open systems model, oriented toward network forms of interaction, in which power is dispersed and fluid, and the actors are interdependent on each other's resources, the focus being on innovation and change allowing adaptation to new challenges.

4. The self-governance model, oriented toward long-term gains and focusing on building sustainability by fostering relationships of interdependence and reciprocity.

While Newman's models are based on the changing panorama of British governance, they are relevant to an examination of governance in Japan as they include all the facets of functioning liberal democracies.

Although it is hard to classify Japan into any one of the above four models, the authors wish, nevertheless, to use them in order to explain the background and the changes that have contributed to transformations in Japan's governance.

The hierarchical model is prevalent, the centralized administration of the state having been imbued with a paternalistic power, characterized by protection and equity considerations. International relations have been the exclusive preserve of the Ministry of Foreign Affairs and central government departments, while the community has been important only in the context of economic revitalization policies. With all the decision-making authority vested in the central government, the rational goal model could also be seen in the workings of Japan's iron triangle, the government-business-interest group relationship.

Nevertheless, the facts we have identified are more aligned with the open systems and self-governance models. The transformations we are currently witnessing in Japan's governance are pole opposites to those so bitterly deplored by critics in the past. The drift has been away from an antistatist to a more democratic orientation, as the authority of both government and big business has weakened and the accountability of both institutions has been eroded. Scandals are abundant, and doubts have been cast on the effectiveness of public and business policies. Against this background, it has become necessary to ensure the integrity of society using other actors and institutions such as civil society organizations, local governments, and think tanks. These institutions can best integrate a fragile and transient society by providing a coherent set of values, a role once borne by public organizations. Japan is full of public sector–related organizations, in which the term public has the connotation of good and supreme. The increasingly pluralistic political environment, more competitive business scene, and more numerous citizen engagements have contributed to building new institutions, as a result of which interaction involving the government and citizens has become even more of a prerequisite of the public policymaking process. After all, the provision of public service is not a monopoly of the government but, rather, of a network of actors.

## INSTITUTIONS

Traditional interpretations of Japanese governance tend to explain it as a product of a "unique" society, and the fast economic growth of past decades has often been attributed to cultural uniqueness. Specialists in Japan will often be heard to say that Japan is a unique country, characterized by non-Western culture and customs, in which Japanese people behave in a way that is beyond the ken of Westerners. Further, they will explain, in Japan the relationship between the state and the market is different, as the state exerts a formidable power that shapes the market and the life of the people: government is not authoritarian, society is comparatively regulated, and philanthropies of significance are few.

But such claims do not preclude any meaningful comparison. Thus Ezra Vogel, in his best-selling book *Japan as Number One* (1979), intended not to praise Japan's success but, rather, to suggest that American policymakers and business leaders alike might do well to adopt Japan's best practices. Two decades later, while its American counterparts have learned to manage the economy, Japan finds itself in the grip of a protracted recession. Clearly, although Vogel's contentions were not identical with those of the social theorists who claim that Japan is unique, they did reinforce the theorists' view.

Culture, however, is not the only factor that sets Japan apart from other societies. Less visible but, nevertheless, important are its constitutional and governmental structures, and the rules and customs that set the framework to shape the behavior of actors in the societal, political, and economic arenas.

As March and Olsen (1995, 28) explain, first, human actions are driven less by the anticipation of uncertain consequences and personal preferences for these consequences than by a logic of appropriateness reflected in a structure of rules and perceptions of identity. Second, ever-changing historical reality matches institutions, behaviors, and contexts in ways that have multiple, path-dependent levels of equilibrium. Third, governance extends beyond negotiating coalitions within given constraints of rights, rules, preferences, and resources, shaping those constraints and allowing meaningful perceptions of politics, history, and the self to be constructed.

While Peters (2000) uses seven identifiers to track the development of governance and the associated institutions, he, too, traces the roots of the newly evolving institutionalism to the above three-point formulation. For, he says, under such an institutional framework, people act in what is considered to be an appropriate, rational fashion. The corporate world will, thus, become rapidly attuned to changes in the global market and governance in order to survive, as will the political parties in power to the political marketplace. In other words, the political shaping of society presupposes a common set of institutions.

Consequently, it can be said that clearly defined challenges will naturally allow appropriate actions to be taken, as a result of which rules and institutions will gradually change. Since institutions set the framework for the behavior and actions of their respective participants and society as a whole, any institutions that are structurally different from others will produce in their society patterns of behavior that are, likewise, different. It is, thus, the institutions that make Japan appear to be unique, for as governance is transformed, institutions and the rules of the game will inevitably change.

Chapter one of this volume takes a look at the challenges facing Japan's decentralization strategy, with Furukawa Shun'ichi focusing on the new relationship between the central government and local governments that developed in the 1990s and culminated in the 1999 Omnibus Law of Decentralization. As Furukawa points out, the main thrust of this law is, through the abolition of the notorious agency-delegated function system, to decrease central government control over local affairs.

In a half century during which time there has been a steady democratization of the state and local governments have achieved a degree of autonomy that has allowed them to manage their own public policy—including regional development, welfare, the environment, and information disclosure—there have been vast changes in overall national policy and governance. The current decentralization strategy is, in fact, another step in the evolution of local autonomy, reflecting as it does reforms that have been under way for almost ten years.

Besides a detailed description of legislative procedure, the process of decentralization is tackled from three angles: changes in relations between the central government and local governments, administrative reform, and the realization of democratic principles. These perspectives are then used to show how Japan's institutional setting makes it possible for local governments to step in and get the job done when the central government hits a policy deadlock. It is this leadership model, based on local government initiative, that provides the litmus test for government.

In chapter two, Kanagawa Kōji analyzes the recent surge of community business which, although new in Japan, has already made a mark on local communities. The government's failure to provide adequate services has led to an increase in NPOs, which are often characterized by working styles that are not necessarily traditional. Thus it is that the entry of women into the labor market and the growing number of the post-retirement elderly has created a new type of workplace: the community business. Neither for-profit nor nonprofit, and owned and controlled by the community as a whole, this kind of enterprise originated in the United Kingdom where charities have long been prevalent. Several examples of this type of community business are described, together with the support provided by local government.

In chapter three, Kashiwazaki Chikako gives a comprehensive overview of internationalization programs being put in place that relate to foreign residents of Japan. Despite the move to accommodate greater diversity in society, there is as yet no consensus on policy as it pertains to foreign residents. Four local-level government responses highlight the basis of this policy and the social services available in the foreign-resident programs that represent the internationalization-from-within aspect of Japan's policy of internationalization, as distinct from its national policy. Internationalization-from-within is being adopted as a policy to revitalize localities by assisting foreign residents to participate in public life.

Another perspective on changing local government policy is presented in chapter four, in which Menju Toshihiro discusses some of the international policies of local governments. International exchange has been a common agenda for many local governments throughout the last four decades, having begun in the mid-1950s with the sister-city relationship that quickly attracted the attention of local leaders desperate to be involved in the international arena. Over the years, the simple exchange programs have become more meaningful and effective. One example is the Japan Exchange and Teaching (JET) Programme, in place since 1987. Despite its various problems (McConnel 2000), it now has over 6,000 participants from more than 30 countries and has evolved into the biggest international exchange program. In the 1990s, Japan became interested in international cooperation and focused on overseas development assistance (ODA), a type of cooperation program that was also implemented at the local level.

But Japan's international policy faces numerous challenges, including the absence of strategy, its lack of specialists, the need to collaborate with NPOs, and the need to modernize its sister-city affiliations. Nonetheless, opportunities also exist. Japan's international policy can become more independent from the central government, compatible with the private sector, better attuned to a multi-ethnic environment, and more helpful to the Third World.

As Nakamura Madoka points out in chapter five, the term think tank bears a different connotation in the Japanese setting—where for-profit research institutes are dominant—than it does in other societies. As the regional- and local-government policy processes have been changing recently, think tanks based in localities have gained importance. Starting with a comparison of what is implied by the term in major countries, the role of think tanks in the regional policy process is examined. Whereas in the past the relationship between local governments and think tanks suffered due to a dearth of expertise and overdependence on contract research, the recent transformation of the regional policy process and increased competition have resulted in a more favorable environment for the development of regional think tanks. The expansion of think tank networks and university-affiliated policy institutes, as well as the advent of flourishing community-based think tanks has resulted in the accommodation of this transformation. The new type of policy process involving think tanks appears promising in the new system of governance.

Missing in the most recent decentralization scheme is an agenda of public finance reform that addresses questions concerning the allocation of functions and resources and the implementation of a coherent system of accountability. Without the reallocation of tax and independent revenue sources, fiscal accountability in local government will not be complete. As does chapter one, Numao Namiko argues in chapter six for more revenue sources to allow ailing local public finances to be more viable and accountable. While intergovernmental fiscal relations have not been neglected in Japan, the national treasury's recent heavy deficits have tended to discourage the reallocation of tax revenues. The central government shares with local governments most sources of tax income and expenditure, a system that is further complicated by the local allocation tax revenue-sharing scheme. The most recent amendments of the revenue-raising capacity of local governments are explained and arguments made for more autonomous decision making.

Chapter seven by Tamura Shigeru highlights another important theme: the development of NPOs in Japan and their relationship with local governments, a theme that is directly related to the issue of governance. In the wake of the 1995 Great Hanshin-Awaji Earthquake in western Japan, a volunteer sector suddenly appeared and led to the enactment of the 1998 Law to Promote Specified Nonprofit Activities (NPO Law) that authorizes the incorporation of NPOs. As a result, NPOs have become increasingly involved in such areas as welfare, international exchange, and community affairs, despite their fragile revenue structure and inadequate tax-exempt status. So it is that today, local governments are even keen to collaborate with NPOs, since such cooperation enhances the viability of public policy and its implementation.

## BIBLIOGRAPHY

Johnson, Chalmers. 1995. *Japan:Who Governs? The Rise of the Developmental State*. New York: W.W. Norton.

Kettle, Donald F. 1993. *Sharing Power: Public Governance and Private Markets*. Washington, D.C.: Brookings Institution Press.

March, James G., and Johan P. Olsen. 1995. *Democratic Governance*. New York: Free Press.

McConnel, David L. 2000. *Importing Diversity: Inside Japan's JET Programme*. Berkeley, Calif.: University of California Press.

Newman, Janet. 2001. *Modernising Governance: New Labour, Policy and Society*. London: Sage.

Peters, B. Guy. 2000. *Institutional Theory in Political Science: The New Institutionalism*. London: Pinters.

Pierre, Jon, ed. 2000. *Debating Governance*. Oxford, U.K.: Oxford University Press.

Pierre, Jon, and B. Guy Peters. 2000. *Governance, Politics and the State*. London: Macmillan.

Rhodes, R.A.W. 1997. *Understanding Governance: Policy Networks, Governance, Reflexivity and Accountability*. Buckingham, U.K.: Open University Press.

Salamon, Lester M., and Helmut K. Anheier. 1996. *The Emerging Sector*. Manchester, U.K.: Manchester University Press.

Salamon, Lester M. et al. 1999. *Global Civil Society: Dimensions of the Nonprofit Sector*. Baltimore, Md.: The Johns Hopkins Center for Civil Society Studies.

Strange, Susan. 1996. *The Retreat of the State: The Diffusion of Power in the World Economy*. Cambridge, U.K.: Cambridge University Press.

Vogel, Ezra F. 1979. *Japan as Number One: Lessons for America*. Cambridge, Mass.: Harvard University Press.

Wolferen Karel van. 1989. *The Enigma of Japanese Power*. London: Macmillan.

Yamamoto Tadashi, ed. 1995. *Emerging Civil Society in the Asia Pacific Community*. Tokyo: Japan Center for International Exchange.

———, ed. 1998. *The Non-profit Sector in Japan*. Manchester, U.K.: Manchester University Press.

# Japan's Road to Pluralism

# 1

# Decentralization in Japan

## Furukawa Shun'ichi

The democratization that took place in Japan over the latter half of the twentieth century led to local governments achieving a degree of autonomy that allowed them to manage aspects of public policy in such areas as regional development, welfare, environmental protection, and government information disclosure. As these local authorities increasingly became active players in the policymaking process, rather than mere central government agents, they came to influence national public policy and governance. The subsequent decentralization reforms are part of the broader public-sector reforms of the 1990s.

During the last decade of the twentieth century, the government of Japan achieved a significant degree of decentralization, the high point of which was the 1999 Omnibus Law of Decentralization. As a result, a new relationship was established among the branches of government, with the central government ceding some control over local affairs. This chapter assesses the degree of decentralization achieved to date, as well as the challenges that await those seeking further decentralization.

## THE ADMINISTRATION

In this country of 47 prefectures, some 3,200 municipal governments
serve a population of 126 million. The central government is divided
into executive, legislative, and judicial branches. The executive branch
comprises the prime minister and his cabinet; the legislative branch,
the Diet or bicameral parliament; and the judicial branch, the Supreme
Court, under which there are no specialized courts.

Local self-government, guaranteed by the Constitution of 1947,
provides for directly elected governors, mayors, and assembly members. At the local-government level, authorities have a wide range of
functions and fiscal responsibilities; a fusion of responsibility and finance exists, with two-thirds of all government expenditure being local; and there is a tradition of frequent personnel shifts at the executive
level (Furukawa 1999). Until March 2000, local governments were
bound by the agency-delegated function (ADF) system, according to
which they were expected to implement functions delegated by the
central government agencies. Designed originally to help achieve quick
post–World War II economic recovery, the system more recently had
the effect of diluting responsibility in government and eroding local
autonomy. Rigid financial control by the central government propped
up this fusion of functions, with roughly 70 percent to 80 percent of
prefectural responsibility and 30 percent to 40 percent of municipal
government functions having fallen within this ADF category. The
promise to the bureaucracy of financial security had guaranteed tight
central control and so, as of August 2000, there were in office more
than 1,600 elite bureaucrats who had been recruited from the central
government for such local authority posts as that of vice-governor,
deputy mayor, and departmental head (data from the Ministry of
Public Management, Home Affairs, Posts and Telecommunications,
*Asahi Shimbun* 30 March 2001).

## THE ISSUES

### Decentralization

Worldwide, decentralization is a recent phenomenon that has been
fostered by the spread of democratization, growing cultural and ethnic

identification, and the trend toward globalization, which is a critical factor in Japan's decentralization process. Nevertheless, one should recognize that, while globalization exposes the smaller regions of the world to the global marketplace, its values may take precedence over local values so that, when a country's political, economic, and developmental activities become globalized, the national government may cease to be dominant.

Globalization has created new, complex networks that are different from the former centralized system (Jun and Wright 1996) and, in many countries, this has required new institutional settings, one result of which is decentralized administration. In such cases, globalization has enhanced local governance and subsidiarity, as can be seen from the International Union of Local Authorities' famous 1985 WorldWide Declaration on Local Self-Government.

In Japan, democratization, globalization, and public-sector reform have contributed most to decentralization. Matsumoto Hideaki (2000), himself a noted executive bureaucrat and major actor in the decentralization process, stresses that a centralized system is not only irrelevant to an affluent society, but may even be detrimental to its development. Instead, he emphasizes such goals as independent decision making and individual responsibility. Kitamura Wataru (2000), meanwhile, argues that the political and economic changes that have recently occurred in Japan as a result of international impetus are a "coalition of decentralization," involving business and local government. This is the result of the desire of the business sector to have a more flexibly managed regional economic policy, so that local authorities have greater discretionary power.

The social system developed in Japan in the wake of World War II was no different from the "1940 System" (Noguchi 1995), which prescribed protectionist and paternalistic public policies, especially in the areas of banking, finance, and industry. Ironically, the factors now accelerating decentralization in Japan are no different from those that contributed to the end of an earlier system.

## Intergovernmental Relations

The term central-local government relations is often used in reference to the centralized-decentralized and fused-separate dimensions between the central government and local authorities. It is generally believed that Japan's central-local relations are centralized-fused (Amakawa 1986). The concept of intergovernmental relations, dominant in the United States, denotes the interactions between various levels of government, including the executive branch, as well as comprehensive relations in a political setting (Wright 1988; Rhodes 1999).

Muramatsu Michio (1997), in his study on intergovernmental relations in Japan, identifies three models: the vertical administration control model, the horizontal political competition model, and the overlapping authority model.

The vertical administration control model, or centralization paradigm, has its basis in the period 1945–1955, when Japan was rebuilding after World War II; it is the traditional arrangement of intergovernmental relations in which local governments occupy the subordinate position.

The horizontal political competition model, meanwhile, includes elements of the vertical administration control model as well as of the central-local political structure created by politicians. This model, which originated in Japan's regional development policy of the 1960s and 1970s, suggests a two-way process. It is also a step toward the interdependent relationship seen in the third, overlapping authority model in which functions are delegated by the central government to be implemented by local governments.

Political advocacy for decentralization often reflects the vertical administration control model, in which local governments find themselves in a disadvantageous position. This line of thinking, which has become assimilated in politics and administration, is not illogical, but the issue is more complex than it would first appear. Horizontal competition and interdependence are involved as politicians tend not to foster decentralization, in the belief that politics is already adequately decentralized. So, for example, most members of the Diet will be more concerned with negotiating a favorable status for their districts in resource allocation. Thus, while the overlapping authority model might be a persuasive interpretation of the reality of the welfare state, it has not found good friends in politics and administration.

## Administrative Reform

Central-local government relations has been one of the focal points of past administrative reforms due to the interrelated nature of Japan's system of government. An evaluation of the post–World War II administrative reforms reveals four distinct periods (Furukawa 1999): the democratic phase (from 1945 to the 1950s), the management-oriented phase (from the 1960s to the 1970s), the liberal conservative phase (in the 1980s), and the reorganization phase (in the 1990s). In each of these periods, decentralization was on the reform agenda, even though accomplishments to that end were meager (Jun and Mutō 1998).

The first reform phase, following Japan's defeat in World War II, was marked by a fundamental change to public administration; postwar reforms sought to promote efficiency and a more democratic orientation. In 1947, the then-Ministry of the Interior—which had been in charge of the country's police force, local administrative bodies, and public works—was divided into eight separate organizations. One significant effect of this move was that prefectural governors were thereafter elected by direct popular vote, rather than appointed by the central government, thus altering the balance of power in the administrative and political arenas. This led other central government departments to establish regional offices for the administration of local matters that, although long under the jurisdiction of prefectures, had formerly been controlled by the Ministry of the Interior. The work of local and regional administrations was, thus, duplicated and fragmented.

Most of the recommendations emerging from the second, management-oriented reform phase of the 1960s and 1970s were not implemented as intended, although the central bureaucracy was somewhat reduced and several public corporations were merged. Unfortunately, while curbs were placed on the size of the civil service at the national level, it expanded at the local level and special public corporations soon appeared. With the subsequent increase in local government personnel, justified on the grounds that numerous functions had been delegated by the central government, it appeared that local governments had assumed greater responsibility. But the reality was that their discretionary powers had been reduced; political scientists of the day cynically spoke of a "new centralization," not unlike Muramatsu's classic vertical administration control model (1997, 21).

Although the two oil crises of the 1970s resulted in a national deficit amounting to more than 30 percent of the government's annual revenue, the introduction of a sales or consumption tax was strongly

opposed by the business community, which sought fiscal restructuring without a tax increase. Thus in 1981, at the start of the third, liberal
conservative phase of administrative reform, the Second Provisional
Commission on Administrative Reform was established to promote
cutbacks in management and the devolution of power to local government authorities. Both the Ministry of Finance and the Ministry of
Home Affairs cooperated in this effort, but progress was limited, even
though the spending cuts and increased privatization of the then-three
biggest public corporations—the Japan National Railway, Nippon
Telegraph and Telephone Public Corporation, and Japan Tobacco and
Salt Public Corporation—have been claimed as major victories of the
administrative reforms of the day. In short, there was little change in
central-local relations.

In the fourth, reorganization phase of reforms that took place in the
1990s, central government departments were reorganized into one
cabinet office and twelve ministries and agencies. It was only then that
the major decentralization of government really began.

## A Reform Model

Administrative reform is based on four factors, namely, driving forces,
the political system, the administrative system, and the interface of
the political and administrative systems. This breakdown is a revision
of that of Christopher Pollitt and Geert Bouckaert (2000, 26), which
addresses general factors affecting reform in ten countries, mainly in
Europe and not including Japan.

In the case of Japan, the driving forces factor has two components.
The first is a socioeconomic element that involves systemic change
and is influenced by globalization, the aging society, economic recession, and regional economic disparity. The second is a political element
that involves reform and is influenced by pressure from citizens and
the media to rectify mismanagement and instances of malfeasance as
well as bad policy.

The second factor on which administrative reform is based is the
political system, and it includes such considerations as party politics
and political realignment. Decentralization has produced an ideological division between the long-dominant, conservative Liberal Democratic Party (LDP) and the opposition parties. Ever since the LDP

developed a congenial relationship with the central bureaucracy, centralization has seemed the preferable alternative, while the opposition parties, which had until recently been excluded from power, were drawn to the progressive local governments which were effective in the quest for control of the central government.

This was particularly true in the 1960s and 1970s, when most metropolitan prefectures and cities had governors and mayors supported by opposition parties. Comprising mainly socialists and communists, the opposition saw greater decentralization as a means of enhancing their political base. Since the LDP was otherwise inclined, however, the result was an even more rigid administrative system—the third factor on which administrative reform was based—that allowed the ruling party to exert centrally regulated legal and fiscal power over local governments.

The resultant administrative system proved an unusually productive moment in the political life of Japan, for the reforms conformed to the specific organizational interests and the elite bureaucrats were thus engaged in not only designing the strategy, but also enhancing the results, including the privatization of government enterprises and spending cuts, which behavior is comparable to the bureau-shaping model put forward by Patrick Dunleavy (1991).

The fourth factor on which administrative reform was based, namely, the interface of the political and administrative systems, is the connecting point of the two key facets of government: It is crucial to understanding the nature of a bureaucratic state.

## THE LEGISLATIVE PROCESS

### The 1995 Law for Promoting Decentralization

The 1990s witnessed Japan's first major political realignment in forty years. The process began in 1992, when the Japan New Party under Hosokawa Morihiro—a former Kumamoto prefecture governor who hailed from a family of the highest prewar aristocracy—won four seats in the Diet's House of Councillors (Upper House) election. The first priority of the Japan New Party was decentralization, which Hosokawa deemed important based on his gubernatorial experience. The election results were supportive of his stance and, making an impact in those political circles aware of the effectiveness of this platform, set in motion the trend that followed.

Hosokawa was, from 1990 to 1992, a member of the Third Provisional Council for the Promotion of Administrative Reform (1990–1993), which in 1992 issued a recommendation for decentralization. This was met, as had been the original plan of 1991, with formidable opposition from the ruling LDP and the bureaucracy, as a result of which almost nothing was achieved. Following this experience, Hosokawa decided that creating a new, viable political party would be the quickest way to achieve decentralization.

The concept of decentralization became common parlance in the political arena only when, just before the House of Representatives (Lower House) election in June 1993, both houses of the Diet passed almost identical bipartisan resolutions on decentralization calling for appropriate legislation. A new political phase had started.

Diet resolutions are not generally binding but, as reflections of the political environment, are instrumental in agenda setting. In this case, however, political actors and scholars alike agree that the resolutions were epoch-making (Matsumoto 2000). Decentralization had been in gridlock for years, caught up in administrative reforms and blocked by the opposition in the compartmentalized bureaucracy, but the resolutions underlined the importance of decentralization.

The long dominance of the LDP ended in 1993, and the new coalition government, headed by Hosokawa, placed decentralization on its political agenda. In October 1993, the Third Provisional Council for the Promotion of Administrative Reform handed to its former member, Hosokawa, its final recommendations on decentralization that included a basic plan. Despite different configurations, coalition governments have since been the rule in Japan, and it was one such government, led by Socialist Prime Minister Murayama Tomiichi (1994–1996), that in May 1995 enacted the Law for Promoting Decentralization. The law did not, however, include provisions for the decentralization of government functions and finance, its major component being the establishment of the Committee for the Promotion of Decentralization (CPD), which proved to be an effective organ for the deciding of strategy and its implementation.

Four main factors made it possible for the Decentralization Law to be enacted. First, the prefectural and municipal authorities cooperated, and various recommendations—notably one made in October 1993 by the Third Provisional Council for the Promotion of Administrative Reform—ensured that the two-tiered local government system would continue.

Second, the existence of a coalition government and the configuration of its actors contributed to the requisite flexibility and compromise. The LDP, a coalition partner from 1994, was not enthusiastic about decentralization, but the Socialist Party and Sakigake (Pioneer) Party, also coalition partners, were convinced that decentralization was critical to the policy agenda and stood their ground. Since the LDP needed the cooperation of coalition partners in order to stay in power, it chose to compromise.

Third, the decentralization cause had the support of important political figures: Murayama, the prime minister, formerly a member of a prefectural assembly, who was supported by Jichirō (All-Japan Prefectural and Municipal Workers Union); Igarashi Kōzō, his chief cabinet secretary and a Socialist Party member, who had once been a city mayor; Takemura Masayoshi, chief of the Sakigake Party, finance minister and former chief cabinet secretary under Hosokawa, who had been a city mayor and prefectural governor before entering the Lower House; Nonaka Hiromu, LDP leader and home minister, who was a former mayor, prefectural assembly member, and vice-governor of Kyoto; and, standing between politics and the bureaucracy, Ishihara Nobuo, the deputy chief cabinet secretary appointed from the bureaucracy and former vice-home minister, who had served more than seven years in the bureaucratic hierarchy and could exert effective coordinative power over the central departments.

Japan's policy process in the central government revolves around decisions taken by the cabinet, which proposes over 80 percent of the bills submitted to the Diet. Most major decisions in the cabinet thus require consensus among its members and those of the ruling coalition parties. Thus, having placed key actors in the cabinet, the Murayama administration was able to finalize decisions on decentralization and, despite negative attitudes within the LDP and the bureaucracy, the interface of political and administrative systems—the fourth factor on which administrative reform was based—functioned well.

A policy window, as in John W. Kingdon's model (1995), opened as the LDP's long-standing dominance in Japanese politics ended.

Without this political realignment, the window would have remained shut, given the LDP was loath to pursue decentralization.

A fourth factor that made possible the enactment of the Decentralization Law is the balance of power in the administrative system. Developments became possible with the cooperation of the Ministry of Home Affairs, local government associations, and scholars closely linked to the Murayama administration. In September 1994, six local government associations had put forward the Guidelines for Promoting Decentralization. Meanwhile, the recommendations and proposals made by the government administrative reform headquarters and research committees were almost identical, most of the membership of the bodies overlapping. When the Ministry of Home Affairs exerted particular influence on the recommendations, causing other ministries to become not a little suspicious, the responsibility for drafting the bill was allotted to the Management and Coordination Agency, which was in charge of administrative reform. Counterattacks from the other ministries were thereby blunted until deliberations began at the CPD.

## Deliberation at the CPD

In an attempt to preempt powerful intervention behind the scenes, the commission assumed a mantle of openness and deliberations were made public soon after each meeting. However, Murayama resigned in 1996, in the wake of difficulties encountered in connection with policy issues ranging from matters relating to the Great Hanshin-Awaji Earthquake of January 1995 to antirecession measures following the bursting of the economic bubble. Speculation was that the new coalition administration of Hashimoto Ryūtarō, LDP president, would not be as enthusiastic about decentralization as had been its predecessor.

But reform-related deliberation proceeded, albeit characterized by traditional, compartmentalized, interdepartmental rivalries and time-consuming negotiations with the CPD, since the new administration's resolve concerning decentralization was somewhat less focused. It should be remembered that the CPD, an advisory organ, was acting in the capacity of bureaucratic member organization of the cabinet, as a result of which its zeal for decentralized administration met opposition from central government organizations that feared the decentralization scheme would merely serve to enhance the power of the

Ministry of Home Affairs, which was in charge of intergovernmental relations. Ministries thus mobilized politicians who favored centralized administration for the political influence it allowed over resource allocation. For the CPD and these ministries to reach an agreement necessitated compromise.

Prime Minister Hashimoto (1996–1998) was more inclined to tackle the administrative reforms pertaining to the reorganization of the central government. Scandals involving high-ranking bureaucrats in major ministries plagued his administration, and failures of public policy, particularly as regards banking, created distrust of the once-respected bureaucracy. On November 21, 1996, amid calls for accountability, the Hashimoto cabinet established the Administrative Reform Council, the remit of which was the reorganization of the central government.

Hashimoto, a conservative reformer, did not have a substantial political base in his party, having been elected to its presidency only because he had been instrumental in boosting popular support in the coalition government. Philosophically, he was drawn to the doctrine of state supremacy and feared an increase in the local power of governors although, as leader of the coalition government, he did agree to foster the course of action launched by the Murayama cabinet.

The CPD believed that Hashimoto would give the nod to its recommendations, which would not include those with which he disagreed. Four recommendations were thus presented to Hashimoto in 1996 and 1997 and, in May 1998, the cabinet consolidated them into the Decentralization Plan.

## Decentralizing Public Works and the 1999 Omnibus Law of Decentralization

The Law of Reorganization of Central Ministries and Agencies was enacted in 1998 with reorganization having started in January 2001, and, even though some ministries have been consolidated or renamed, their basic structure remains virtually unchanged. While most agencies with ministerial portfolios have been merged, there will continue to be twelve ministries. But the bigger ministries will be too large to control unless a substantial number of functions are devolved to local government, a fear that has been confirmed by the disappointing devolution results to date.

As plans for central government reorganization unfolded in 1997, Hashimoto wanted to streamline the Ministry of Land, Infrastructure and Transportation, which would soon encompass the four major public works organizations. These organizations accounted for more than 8 percent of Japan's gross domestic product (GDP), a figure that is two to four times larger than that of other advanced countries. The prospects of having a leviathan ministry drew a great deal of criticism, since without substantial devolution to local authorities, particularly at the prefectural level, there would be significant risk of its being uncontrollable and prone to exerting political pressure on elected politicians—a fear that has already materialized.

When the CPD was drafting its fifth recommendation, which the public works bureaucracy opposed strongly, politicians were again mobilized and the vice-minister for construction publicly announced his opposition. In the meantime, Hashimoto had to resign due to party setbacks in the Upper House election in July 1998. The final CPD recommendations, submitted in November 1998 to Obuchi Keizō (1998–2000), who succeeded Hashimoto as prime minister, were unsatisfactory as regards terms for devolution. Vested opposition interests prevailed and local governments were divided, fearing that devolution would decrease their grants. As a result, the fifth recommendation saw changes only in the areas pertaining to city planning and the consolidation of grants to municipal governments, which was scaled down. Counterbalancing the agreed-upon decentralization, however, was the construction industry, which accounts for more than 10 percent of the country's labor force, a figure that is twice as large as that of major Western countries. Four recommendations had been incorporated into the Decentralization Plan of May 1998.

Taking the content of these five viable recommendations together, the Diet enacted the Omnibus Law of Decentralization in July 1999, which took effect in April 2000. The legislative process was complex in the extreme, with 475 laws, 440 cabinet orders, 507 ministerial orders, and 186 public notices. The eight major components of the law are: the clarification of the roles of the state and local governments; the abolition of the ADF system; deregulation of the jurisdiction of local affairs; the creation of mechanisms for mediating disputes between central and local governments; the devolution of sixty-four functions;

the creation of "special cities" with populations of over 200,000 that would enjoy still greater devolution from prefectures; the deregulation of requirements for establishing offices and organizations in local governments; the consolidation of grants-in-aid and an increase in the discretionary taxing power of local governments.

Reform of the local government system touches on three areas. The first is the overhauling of the basic framework of local authorities' functions. In addition to abolition of the ADF system, the law stipulates a new classification of local functions either as those that are autonomous or those that are entrusted by law. The latter are defined as functions administered by local governments but regulated by national law or cabinet order to ensure proper implementation.

The second area is the need for less central control. Since local governments already implement most domestic functions, the law is not specific, but city planning is cited as an example of an area requiring significant devolution, and a general reduction in central government intervention and involvement is emphasized, with new rules established for central-local government relations.

The third area is devolution from prefectural governments. Communities with a population exceeding a certain figure are granted wider functions, which has led to the diversification of municipal government.

## DECENTRALIZATION EVALUATED

Evaluation has not been uniform. For example, the chairman of the CPD hailed the decentralization scheme as a major step toward viable governance. As a major actor in the process, the chairman described local government reforms as the "third revolution," after the Meiji Restoration of 1868 and the nation's post-1945 democratization. Other actors involved in the process have also tended to see the strategy favorably. Matsumoto (2000) concurs that it has resulted in more genuine local autonomy—as stipulated in Article 92 of the constitution —by redefining central local relations as independent decision making and individual responsibility. Nishio Masaru (2000), a leading member of the CPD, sees the strategy as an "unfinished revolution."

Law professors also saw the abolition of the ADF system as a positive step, complaining only about the inadequate fiscal-legal framework (Kaneko 1999).

Political scientists, however, have been more ambivalent. For example, Matsushita Keiichi (1999), a long-time Social Democratic Party ideologue, claims that while the decentralization scheme provides impetus for an autonomous, decentralized system, it still leaves local governments facing many challenges, including fiscal stress, the hollowing out of assemblies, insufficient government information disclosure, and a degrading public policy. Muramatsu (1999) is less enthusiastic in his evaluation, noting that reform is but a natural course of action designed to authorize the current authorities' ability and postwar performance.

In light of these responses, this writer proposes three perspectives whereby to evaluate the decentralization strategy: changes in central-local relations, reform of the administrative system, and realization of democratic principles.

## Changes in Central-Local Relations

Muramatsu's typology (1997) depicts the chronological progress from the vertical administration control model to the horizontal political competition model, with the current situation explained by the interdependent overlapping authority model. Viewed against the new decentralized framework, these models bear reexamination.

First, the issue regarding the legal interpretation of the new system was whether and to what extent the federal principle can and should be incorporated into a unitary state. Under an American type of federal system, the central government only exercises such power as is granted by the constitution, while the states hold the residual power. While the first recommendation of the CPD states that proposed limitations shall be the "principle for legislation," in the Omnibus Law of 1999 this wording was changed to "consideration for legislation." If limitations should be the principle, then the governmental system would eventually be similar to a federal system. But as there have been no strong historical and ethnic factors necessitating power sharing between central and local governments, an orientation toward establishing a federal system in Japan was avoided through use of the less normative compromise wording "consideration for legislation."

This writer once proposed a "substantial federal system" (Furukawa 1993) that can be realized under the current constitution. This idea is unrelated to legal arguments and suggests merely a reorganization of the administrative system. A substantial federal system can be achieved by simply reorganizing the central government's branch offices without a constitutional revision. Amalgamation of prefectural governments is another matter altogether. True decentralization cannot be realized through the legal system alone. Relying too much on a legal system, which is actually only a framework, is almost the same as the continental European view of "Rechtsstaat" (legalistic state). This view easily transforms into the "wishful thinking" by which people feel everything would go well if only a legal system is in place.

Second is the political aspect of central-local relations. The pioneering policies of local authorities have influenced national public policy (Reed 1986). Several local policies regarding welfare and the environment, for instance, have been adopted as national programs, although they may have been criticized as too redistributive at the local level. In another instance, the chairman of the Second Provisional Commission on Administrative Reform pointed to administrative reform in a small town as an example of what central government reform should entail. Information disclosure also had its start in municipal government in the first half of the 1980s, and it was not until 1999 that the national law was enacted.

As the political authority of the central government has declined, governance has undergone changes as well. The role of other sectors of society—the private sector, the market, and nonprofit organizations (NPOs)—has increased correspondingly. In this new framework, the vertical administration control model is no longer applicable—although it may still describe one aspect of a specific case—the thrust of the reforms having been the removal of the situations for which this model was most relevant.

The horizontal political competition model, meanwhile, presupposes that politicians will lobby the central government for advantage, but the declining power of the central government automatically diminishes such lobbying, and greater discretionary power and decision-making authority at the local level limits the number of cases to which this model might apply.

The overlapping authority model, however, retains its validity because the new common functions, called "legally contractual functions," are legally established on an equal and contractual basis. Such common functions still account for roughly half the functions administered by local governments, further emphasizing the overlapping, interdependent aspect of the relationship. Arguably, an integrationist model might remain dominant even after the enactment of decentralization legislation, given that the intense relationship between the two levels of government has roots in local political initiatives (Muramatsu 1997, xviii).

A vertical political and administrative competition model can be proposed based on the above discussions since policy competition often results in alternatives being submitted for consideration by major local governments, including those of Tokyo, the prefectures of Mie and Shizuoka, and the cities of Mitaka, in Tokyo, and Yokosuka, in Kanagawa prefecture (see "Citizen Engagement" sidebar).

This new competition model has three prerequisites: political stability based on election results, public confidence in government, and a solid belief in local autonomy; fiscal solvency alone is not enough. Even small local authorities can put forward an exemplary policy for citizen participation—as did Niseko town in Hokkaido (see sidebar) —or for housing aid for earthquake victims—as did Tottori prefecture. While the central government finds itself in yet another fragile coalition, where policymaking seems an elusive task, local governments are exhibiting the ability to make decisions and implement them promptly, and have displayed sufficient authority and gathered enough energy to alter the balance of the central-local relations.

### Reform of the Administrative System

With decentralization part of the broader public-sector reform initiative, the Omnibus Law of 1999 required that sixty-four government functions be devolved to the local level. While the number is small, it should be remembered that, under the ADF system, most domestic functions had already been implemented at the local level. So, of greater interest were the new functions created to satisfy the desire of the central bureaucracy to maintain control over domestic affairs in order to calm the fears of local authorities that they would

Citizen Engagement and Entrepreneurial Programs

---

Citizen participation, or citizen engagement, was not a normal state of affairs in the central government until the legislation of administrative reform in 2000 encouraged the concept of public involvement as a guideline for policymaking and implementation.

The city of Mitaka, in suburban Tokyo, with a population of 167,000, has been innovative in promoting itself as "A City for Tomorrow," and is a member of Cities of Tomorrow, the International Network for Better Local Government—comprised of ten cities around the world—supported by the Bertelsmann Foundation, Germany. Perhaps inspired by successful precedents overseas and the tradition of its planning process management, Mitaka tried to introduce comprehensive citizen involvement in 1999. This was possibly the first case of its kind in Japan. Mitaka called for some 400 volunteer citizens to draft an original plan for the city. A partnership agreement was made between the Citizen Council for Mitaka Plan 21 Project and the city government. Ten working groups were formed. Based on the ideas of dedicated citizens—academics, professionals, and citizens interested in community affairs—a proposal was presented in October 2000. This proposal formed the basis for formulating a Basic Concept and Master Plan for the City. The learning and collaborative process fostered through the discussions was a meaningful experience both for city staff and citizens.

The city of Yokosuka, Kanagawa prefecture, is undertaking similar endeavors. Yokosuka is unprecedented for including citizen engagement in policymaking and policy implementation. It is also famous for its use of information and communication technologies in municipal administration, and has become a role model.

Operating on a smaller scale, but important in terms of citizen engagement, is Niseko, a small ski resort town in Hokkaido. Niseko is the first local authority in Japan to enact a bylaw to include citizen participation in local administration. The town is famous for its citizen-oriented administration with an annual performance report easily understood even by children.

Tottori, the smallest prefecture in Japan with a population of 610,000, decided to provide assistance to victims of the 2000 earthquake in spite of the interpretation of the law that does not allow for direct grants for personal property rehabilitation because natural calamity damage is beyond the responsibility of government. Without support for rebuilding houses in depopulated areas inhabited mostly by elderly residents, the area affected by the earthquake would have deteriorated. The central government did not have a tool to stop the governor's resolution.

---

inherit devolved functions without sufficient fiscal resources to handle them.

The streamlining of the central bureaucracy has, thus, not been achieved, even though central control has been eased. This can be seen from the way in which public works remain regulated, politicians with particular interests in such areas as agriculture, construction, and commerce being eager to thwart the devolution initiative.

While there was little opposition to the overall idea of fostering decentralization and administrative reform, the compartmentalized decision-making process and bureaucratic politics were viewed as a hindrance when it came to specific issues. It was feared that the results would be little more than disagreement between the Ministry of Home Affairs, in charge of local government, and other ministries and agencies.

The fact that there has been insufficient government reform at the center is partly due to the nature of the Japanese political process. The disintegration of government is a reflection of the compartmentalization of the bureaucracy that is often equated with government in Japan. But this disintegration is not necessarily a factor in local government, where leaders are directly elected, the bureaucracy is comparatively weak, and reform strategies are easier to implement, demonstrating the decentralized nature of centralized government and the centralized leadership of local government (Furukawa 2000).

At the local level, the leadership of governors and mayors, often supported by citizens rather than political parties, may result in the success of efforts at autonomous reform. Effective leadership almost always results in the local bureaucracy being more integrated than its counterpart in the central government. It follows, then, that when the authority of the central bureaucracy is challenged, as is currently the case, local initiatives become possible, as with both the breakthrough by prefectures in the area of environmental protection policy during the 1970s, and performance-based management in local government (see "Performance Measurement" sidebar).

Without either a reallocation of tax resources or independent revenue sources, fiscal accountability in local government is limited. Thus, in the foreseeable future, efforts to achieve autonomy for local government will be made by governors and mayors, many of whom have served in the Diet.

## Realization of Democratic Principles

If the democratic principles of independent decision making and individual responsibility are bases of decentralization, how have they been instrumental in the dynamics of policy formulation?

The active involvement of local authorities has not been extensive, their legal and formal involvement having been institutionally limited. Six local government associations have, to date, aggressively participated in the deliberative process, one of their suggested proposals

### Performance Measurement in the Public Sector

Although performance measurement is related to the most recent administrative reform in central government, efforts at performance measurement first started not at the center but at the periphery. Mie prefecture, located in the central part of the country on the Pacific coast and with a population of 1.8 million, began implementing integrated management based on performance measurement in 1995. The aim is to achieve not only cost savings, but also a transformation of the bureaucratic organization culture with the main concept being customer-oriented service delivery.

Shizuoka prefecture, also on the Pacific coast of central Japan and with a population of 3.7 million, initiated another type of strategic management in 1994. This management reform method has come to be applied to the overall restructuring of government, in addition to cutting the number of staff through consolidation, outsourcing, and the use of information technology.

Hokkaido, the most northern prefecture and with a population of 5.7 million, surprised the ministries by carrying out the first reevaluation of public works. Ministries responsible for public works were surprised that a prefecture, as the recipient of public works subsidies that promote local job opportunities, would initiate a performance measure.

These three entrepreneurial endeavors of local governments in Mie, Shizuoka, and Hokkaido influenced the central government's passing in 1998 of the Basic Law for Central Government Reform.

Performance measurement is also related to the monitoring of comprehensive plans and benchmarking practices as an effective tool for improving performance. To achieve the Tokyo Plan 2000, which aims to create an attractive, dynamic Tokyo by 2015, the Tokyo Metropolitan Government, the largest local authority in Japan with a population of more than 12 million, has developed four "Tokyo Policy Measures": (1) create an urban city that facilitates a balanced working and living environment; (2) create a hometown with abundant nature and culture; (3) improve Tokyo's convenience as a city with the smooth interaction of people, goods, and information; and (4) nurture unique and talented human resources.

being a cutback the equivalent of some US$10 billion. Most local governments, however, have taken a wait-and-see attitude and, with the changes that have taken place in recent coalition governments, the CPD has been at a disadvantage and the decentralization of public works has fallen victim to divide-and-rule politics.

Nevertheless, these obstacles should not be exaggerated, as the degree to which decentralization has been achieved can be measured by the number of democratic leaders who have emerged in recent gubernatorial elections. The year 2000 witnessed the surprise landslide victory in Nagano prefecture of Tanaka Yasuo, a popular writer, over the vice governor. Another surprise was the gubernatorial election in Tochigi prefecture, where the three-term incumbent, with no scandals to besmirch his record, lost by a slim margin to the mayor of a small city. Again in March 2001, an independent female candidate became governor of Chiba prefecture, adjacent to Tokyo, after defeating two contenders supported by major parties. While these three prefectures traditionally vote conservative, the three new governors claimed victory based on the citizens' reevaluation of public programs. This was independent decision making at the most decentralized level, where ideological orientation was not an issue. People wanted a way out of the political bottleneck. The first stage of the decentralization process has thus helped to set the political agenda.

## CHALLENGES TO DECENTRALIZATION

### Amalgamation of Municipalities

Related to devolution and fiscal reform, the issue of amalgamating municipal governments has emerged during the past seven years. Two prior efforts at amalgamation decreased the number of municipalities from 71,314 to 15,820 between 1889 and 1890, and from 9,622 to 3,786 between 1953 and 1957. Since then, the trend has slowed, with the number of municipalities at the end of 2000 standing at 3,229.

Past amalgamation policies were instrumental in modernization and economic growth (Furukawa 1997). Now, however, the issue is focused more on management concerns and the decentralization of government. With increased and overloaded functions delegated to municipal governments of various sizes over the past thirty years, many have been incapable of implementing their respective functions, particularly those relating to welfare care for the elderly, a major concern as Japan's society ages increasingly rapidly.

The central government has tried to promote autonomous amalgamation by amending laws so as to include incentives and inviting greater involvement by prefectural authorities. The resistance it has encountered from local assemblies is revealing. The results to date are considered unsatisfactory by policymakers at the center, there having been only thirteen amalgamations over the last fifteen years, involving a mere thirty-eight municipalities. Paternalistic fiscal equalization and the flow of funds to smaller municipal governments are factors that have deterred amalgamation, while the fiscal incentives to promote amalgamation are no more than guarantees that funds can be transferred. And, because the Local Allocation Tax, a shared revenue with strong equalizing elements, tends to benefit smaller municipalities with less fiscal capacity, amalgamation is seen negatively, since it would serve merely to decrease the resources available to these municipalities.

Nevertheless, as the incentive mechanism in the Omnibus Law of 1999 expires in 2005, the central and prefectural governments have spared no efforts to encourage urban and rural local governments to seriously consider amalgamation. This is particularly true both of those local authorities in major metropolitan areas criticized for their fragmented administration, and of fragile governments in geographically disadvantaged areas. The prospects of declining support from Local Allocation Tax may also have helped bring about this change of heart.

In December 2000, a decision was thus made by the cabinet to consolidate municipal governments into 1,000 units, in order to strengthen their fiscal capacities in the interests of boosting administrative efficiency. This amalgamation will not, however, include prefectural governments.

## Reforming Intergovernmental Fiscal Relations

Lacking on the decentralization agenda was intergovernmental fiscal reform. Grants and shared revenues are under paternalistic control, so the issue is how to relate the division of functions and resources on the one hand, and accountability on the other. Included in the revision of the basic fiscal system were measures for raising local taxes and bonds, although few grants were consolidated or abolished. The strategy of the CPD thus was to redefine the system whereby functions were allotted, with fiscal matters—deemed to take a long time to revise —left to the next phase. The CPD hopes that administrative reform may be followed by fiscal reform (Committee for the Promotion of Decentralization 2001), but the central financial situation is now serious. At the end of fiscal year 2001, it was more than US$4.4 trillion in debt, while centrally controlled local finances were at the brink of bankruptcy, with a total debt of US$1.7 trillion. The fiscal year 1999 settled account of local authorities shows that 60 percent of all local governments are in dire straits. The Local Allocation Tax could not begin to meet the shortfall and, as a result of the widespread fiscal exhaustion, the centrally controlled system has begun to erode.

In April 1999, Ishihara Shintarō, a noted writer, was elected governor of Tokyo, the largest local government in the world. In the summer of that year, he boldly unveiled the Tokyo renaissance plan, which includes proposals for tax and financial reform. In February 2000, he proposed that a corporate enterprise tax be levied on large banking institutions that would evade taxation were it based solely on corporate income rather than gross profit. The new plan is expected to boost revenues by approximately US$5 billion over five years. Ishihara's initiative is a serious challenge to the national government, which has so far failed to implement a tax reform program for local governments. As the Local Tax Law and related fiscal laws through which the central government controls fiscal matters were deregulated in April 2000, other local governments have started to search for ways of generating new tax revenue, including from the refuse-disposal industry and atomic energy–related facilities.

Admittedly, public finance is a complex issue, the wide discrepancies between urban and rural fiscal capacities further complicating the issue. Small local governments with fewer resources are often overloaded, so devolving fiscal resources will not be a solution for these authorities, but a reform plan that will satisfy the needs of all is not easily formulated.

The local-central rift again appeared when, after Prime Minister Koizumi Jun'ichirō took office in April 2001, it was proposed that local public spending be cut. Most local governments complained that Koizumi was neglecting the ailing local economies.

The reform of intergovernmental fiscal relations comes under the purview of public-sector reform. At the central government level, rather than on reorganization, interest currently centers on management: efficient and effective performance-oriented administration. Local government reform is what the central government is seeking, because most domestic government functions are administered at the local level. In light of impending decreases in fiscal support by the central government, no small number of local governments have voluntarily taken reform initiatives. The centralized nature of local administrations has made such reform feasible.

## CONCLUSION

After a half century of existence, local autonomy has accomplished much more than was expected at the time of democratization in the late 1940s, when the new constitution was enacted. The pioneering policies and practices of regional development, welfare, the environmental movement, and public-sector management, including government information disclosure, have influenced national public policy and governance. Local authorities have begun to claim independent positions, departing from their former roles as mere agents of the national government. Decentralization in the 1990s took this postwar transformation of central-local relations a step further and reestablished the legal framework.

Paradoxically, the central government is a decentralized unit, composed of compartmentalized ministries, that often stalls when developing meaningful policy. The institutional setting of Japan is such that when the decentralized ministry system leads the central government to a policy deadlock, local governments are able to step in and get the job done.

Coalition government can be expected to be a regular feature of Japanese politics through the first decade of the twenty-first century and, depending on the configuration of the parties and actors, the degree of decentralization will vary. Missing in the most recent decentralization scheme is an agenda for public finance reform that addresses questions regarding the allocation of functions and resources, and the implementation of a system of accountability.

A leadership model based on local government would stimulate central decision making. The old model of central-local relations—where the central government has a monopoly on power and money, and local governments merely engage in policy implementation—has lost its relevance and can no longer be sustained. Given these new circumstances, the horizontal political competition model, which involves local governments requesting grants-in-aid and designation as special cities, is transformed into more dynamic intergovernmental relations. The resulting model can be termed a vertical political and administrative competition model, even as the overlapping authority model continues to exist.

# BIBLIOGRAPHY

Amakawa Akira. 1986. "Henkaku no kōsō" (Ideas for change in the context of regional government). In Ōmori Wataru and Satō Seizaburō, eds. *Nihon no chihō seifu* (Local government in Japan). Tokyo: University of Tokyo Press.

Committee for the Promotion of Decentralization. 2001. "Final Report." 14 June. <http://www8.cao.go.jp/bunken/bunken-iinkai/saisyu/index.html>.

Dunleavy, Patrick. 1991. *Democracy, Bureaucracy, and Public Choice*. Hemel Hempstead, U.K.: Harvester Wheatsheaf.

Furukawa Shun'ichi, ed. 1993. *Renpōsei: Kyūkyoku no chihō bunken* (Federal system: Ultimate decentralization) Tokyo: Gyōsei.

————. 1997. "An Evaluation of the Amalgamation of Municipalities in Japan." Paper presented at the Dissemination Workshop on "Local Governments and Economic Development in Japan: Lessons for Economies Undergoing Decentralization," sponsored by the World Bank. Budapest, Hungary, 27–28 June.

————. 1999. "Political Authority and Bureaucratic Resilience: Administrative Reform in Japan." *Public Management* 1(3): 439–448.

————. 2000. "An Institutional Framework for Japanese Crisis Management." *Journal of Contingencies and Crisis Management* 8(1): 3–14.

Jun, Jon S., and Hiromi Mutō. 1998. "The Politics of Administrative Reform in Japan: More Strategies, Less Progress." *International Review of Administrative Sciences* 64: 195–202.

Jun, Jon S., and Deil S. Wright. 1996. "Globalization and Decentralization: An Overview." In Jon S. Jun and Deil S. Wright, eds. *Globalization and Decentralization: Institutional Contexts, Policy Issues, and Intergovernmental Relations in Japan and the United States*. Washington, D.C.: Georgetown University Press.

Kaneko Hitoshi. 1999. *Shin chihō jichi hō* (New local autonomy law). Tokyo: Iwanami Shoten.

Kingdon, John W. 1995. *Agendas, Alternatives, and Public Policy*. 2nd ed. New York, N.Y.: HarperCollins.

Kitamura Wataru. 2000. "Kikan inin jimu seido no haishi no seiji katei" (Political process of abolishing the agency-delegated function system). *Kōnan Hōgaku* 40(3/4): 473–526.

Matsumoto Hideaki. 2000. *Shōkai chihō jichi seido* (A detailed interpretation of the new local government system). Tokyo: Gyōsei.

Matsushita Keiichi. 1999. *Jichitai wa kawaru ka* (Does local government change?). Tokyo: Iwanami Shoten.

Muramatsu Michio. 1997. *Local Power in the Japanese State*. Berkeley, Calif.: University of California Press.

————. 1999. *Gyōsei gaku kyōkasho* (Political analysis of modern public administration). Tokyo: Yūhikaku.

Nishio Masaru. 2000. *Mikan no kaikaku* (Unfinished reform). Tokyo: Iwanami Shoten.

Noguchi Yukio. 1995. *1940 nen taisei* (1940 system). Tokyo: Tōyō Keizai Shinpō Sha.

Page, Edward C. 1992. *Political Authority and Bureaucratic Power: A Comparative Analysis.* Hemel Hempstead, U.K.: Harvester Wheatsheaf.

Pollitt, Christopher, and Geert Bouckaert. 2000. *Public Management Reform: A Comparative Analysis.* Oxford, U.K.: Oxford University Press.

Reed, Steven R. 1986. *Japanese Prefectures and Policymaking.* Pittsburgh, Penn.: University of Pittsburgh Press.

Rhodes, R. A. W. 1999. *Control and Power in Central-Local Government Relations.* 2nd ed. Aldershot, U.K.: Ashgate.

Wright, Deil S. 1988. *Understanding Intergovernmental Relations.* 3rd ed. Belmont, Calif.: Wadsworth.

# 2

# The Socioeconomic Impact
# of Community Businesses

## Kanagawa Kōji

The prolonged recession in Japan since the collapse of the bubble economy has caused rising unemployment and weakened regional economies. The jobless rate, which stood at 2.1 percent in 1990, had surged to 5.4 percent by May 2002. Low as the latter figure may be in comparison with that of other advanced nations, it has serious implications given Japan's system of lifetime employment and its consequently underdeveloped employment market. As the economy is decentralized, employment will increasingly be tied to local industries and self-sustaining job development rather than big businesses.

Since the government has failed to provide the services required by society as it matures, a need has developed for alternative service providers. Nongovernmental groups, such as nonprofit organizations (NPOs), are helping to furnish the necessary public services, but at the same time, society is making new demands on the workplace: being sought are broader working options for all beyond the usual patterns of full-time or part-time work. In addition to jobs for women, new employment options that allow retirees to work and contribute to their communities are being sought. This chapter looks at the role of community business (CB), a new way of working developed mainly in the United Kingdom that may well help ease Japan's stringent business environment and activate local economies.

## SOCIAL POLICY FRAMEWORK

In the post–World War II era, advanced countries developed state-based welfare systems. To this end, they increased social security–related expenditures, which required a certain level of economic growth. During the global economy's low-growth period that began in the 1970s, the concept of small government took root in some countries. In the United Kingdom, for example, the Conservative government of Prime Minister Margaret Thatcher encouraged privatization, and the severe curtailment represented by public housing expenditure was vigorously promoted. However, the increase in national expenditure was not sufficiently controlled and so, while certain services were no longer provided by the government, state agencies found themselves lumbered with subsidy and contract costs.[1] In other words, the move to smaller government means a change in the provider of social services, but not necessarily that the role of government is reduced.

When compared with the welfare services of other industrially advanced nations, it is clear that Japan's welfare system needs to be expanded. Because Japan was not faced with a low-growth economy before developing a mature welfare system, its social policy has distinct features, namely, the elderly expect to receive care from family members; industrial policy takes precedence over social policy, with the protection of specific industries contributing to low unemployment; and company-provided—rather than public—welfare is the norm, taking the form of such fringe benefits as company-provided housing, house-renting/purchasing assistance, and low-interest loans.

But the system of company welfare, which primarily applies to lifetime employment and seniority-based systems, is beginning to collapse as the policy of prioritizing supplier protection in favor of consumer protection loses national support. And, although the expectation of family support remains strong compared with the levels found in advanced Western nations, even this is weakening. In short, the pre-conditions supporting the welfare system are changing.

## COMMUNITY BUSINESS

### The Concept

As defined by the Community Business Scotland (CBS) Network, a CB is "a trading organization which is set up, owned, and controlled by the local community and which aims to create self-supporting jobs for local people and be a focus for local development" (Kay 2000). CBs use their profits to expand employment or benefit the community in other ways, according to the community's location and interests.

Most CBs in the United Kingdom take the form of charities, many of which are set up as limited companies by guarantee. In Japan, however, not only are public services sometimes provided by for-profit companies—because the law allowing the incorporation of grass-roots NPOs only came into effect in 1998—but it can be difficult to distinguish between for-profit and nonprofit entities. Nonprofit entities do not pay dividends to shareholders and must reinvest any profit in their main nonprofit activity. Profits are defined as being based on business income and are the funds remaining after allocations for overhead and expenses. What makes it difficult to distinguish between for-profit and nonprofit entities is that nonprofits could in effect distribute dividends by paying their employees higher wages and for-profits can choose to pay low dividends to shareholders (Nakajima 1998). Therefore, depending on their line of business, incorporated for-profit organizations can also sometimes be considered CBs in Japan.

### The Structure

Typically, a CB is a trading organization, meaning it does not offer gratuitous services as does a charity; it contributes to unifying a community; and it reinvests its profits in the community (Kay 2000). That said, there is no global, standard framework for CBs. In the United Kingdom, many organizations that qualify as charities have the legal status of a limited company and can take the form of a social cooperative (a workers' cooperative in Continental European countries). Furthermore, some NPOs have a high enterprise income ratio because they run businesses or charge for their services.

The CB concept originated in Ireland and moved to Scotland, where it evolved further. The CB model was developed in the 1980s, primarily to create jobs during a period of high unemployment in the United Kingdom. It focuses on urgent unemployment-related policy, trade activities, home-based enterprises, and employment development (Katō 1999).

According to CBS, in 1997 there existed at least 110 CBs in Scotland, employing 1,095 persons full time and 68 part time, with transactions totaling £13,670,000. This data is not insignificant in a country of only five million people. Moreover, in 1995 the U.K. city of Liverpool, with a population of about 500,000, had 34 CBs employing 130 individuals (Spencer 2000).

## Comparison with Other Concepts

The concept of CB is best understood when compared with familiar business concepts such as venture business, local industry, and NPOs. One feature CBs have in common with these enterprises is meeting consumer needs. A venture business (VB) will generally have access to advanced technology and know-how, and seek to be listed on a stock exchange, although it will not necessarily bring profits to the community. The CB will also stress the importance of flotation, but in addition it will seek to generate employment in the community. As the employment situation deteriorates in Japan, it is becoming increasingly necessary to encourage all organizations to direct their energies to job creation.

In Japan, traditional enterprises in the textile, ceramics, and agriculture-related manufacturing industries are entirely focused on commercial objectives, whereas CBs focus primarily on a social mission. In addition, the former are distributing primarily manufactured goods and the latter are focusing on social services. NPOs, too, chase social objectives rather than profits but, because they do not share their profits with investors, they cannot access the capital markets for financing and, therefore, depend on donations and subsidies. Thus, NPOs

Table 1. Comparison of Venture Businesses, Community Businesses, and Nonprofit Organizations in Japan

|  | Venture Businesses | Specific Local Industries | Community Businesses | Nonprofit Organizations |
|---|---|---|---|---|
| Main purpose | profit | profit | social objectives | social objectives |
| Type of goods | manufactured goods services | manufactured goods | mainly services | mainly services |
| Type of organization | for-profit | for-profit | nonprofit (for-profit) | nonprofit |
| Legal status | incorporated companies | incorporated companies limited companies | incorporated companies limited companies cooperatives specified nonprofit corporations | incorporated foundations incorporated associations specified nonprofit corporations social welfare corporations, etc. |
| Stakeholders | shareholders investors workers | shareholders workers | workers people in the community | donors volunteers workers people in the community |
| Way of financing | investments loans | institutional loans (investments) | government grants private grants loans (donations) (investments) | government grants private grants donations (loans) |

*Source:* Compiled by author.

include a greater number of community members, philanthropists, and volunteers than do for-profit companies (Machida 2000). See table 1 for a comparison of VBs, CBs, and NPOs.

While the NPO does conduct public-benefit activities—some organizations focusing on providing relief for the poor—it does not share its profits with investors, a practice that is generally followed by CBs in the United Kingdom.[2] In addition, some NPOs are operating beyond the community, while CBs generally only serve the local community.

Since it was very hard for NPOs to become incorporated before the 1998 enactment of the Law to Promote Specified Nonprofit Activities, and many limited or incorporated companies have also pursued social objectives, CBs in Japan do not always have the nonprofit type of corporate body. CBs are purpose-oriented organizations, and it is difficult to identify them by their juridical status (e.g., NPO status, corporation, or welfare incorporation body). For example, in the United Kingdom many CBs qualify as charities, but it is said to be very difficult for those from Scotland to obtain charity status in England and Wales. Perhaps this is because most CBs conduct activities in areas in which existing for-profit enterprises do business. These CBs cannot qualify as charity organizations because they do not engage in activities such as those covered by NPOs. Were the requirement that profits not be distributed among the shareholders removed from the prerequisites for classification as a CB, there would be a blurring of the distinction between CBs and for-profit companies, especially service companies working to benefit the community.

## CBs in Action

In Japan, where the government plays a major role in housing development, CB primarily provides social services such as nursing care for the elderly and childcare. And with the recent increase in unemployment, CB is expected to play an expanding role in occupational training. Following is a brief introduction of some CBs that have already generated economic success nationally.

ARETE CHILDCARE SERVICES    Named after Princess Arete, a fairytale heroine, the organization was established in 1994 by three housewives who met at child-rearing classes in Itami city, Hyogo prefecture. The enterprise offers children a classroom, provides temporary childcare, and organizes parenting classes, but its primary focus is on temporary childcare (Matsuura 1998). The children's classes have a low student-teacher ratio, and the company's clientele numbers about 400 individuals who are registered as service recipients, 90 percent of whom are housewives and 10 percent gainfully employed.

Childcare charges were initially set rather low, but have gradually been raised to allow the enterprise to remain in business. In 1997, after attending a venture enterprise school sponsored by the Hyogo prefectural government, the manager incorporated the company and sought investors. However, because the enterprise was not set up as a for-profit organization, the views of those within the organization vary regarding incorporation. Although it is recognized that incorporation would clear the path to obtaining credit and thus reduce personal liability, such a move would also make it more difficult to obtain government subsidies.[3]

NISHI SUMA DANRAN WELFARE NETWORK   This home-visit welfare service organization provides housekeeping services and has been in operation since May 1998. Based in the Nishi Suma area of Kobe city, it has its roots in the Nishi Suma Community Committee, the neighborhood organization in charge of revitalization programs following the Great Hanshin-Awaji Earthquake of 1995.

The organization covers an area of 5 acres and 10,000 households, with a population of some 24,000 people. With a range of activities that are narrower in scope than those of the average home-visit welfare service, it operates on a membership basis, the members comprising supporters who offer their services, users who benefit from the services, and those members who provide financial support. In February 2002, there was a combined total of 216 supporters and users, and 46 financial support members. Some members of the staff are full-time employees and others volunteers. Service users are charged ¥600 per hour, of which the support staff members' remuneration is ¥500, which leaves ¥100 per hour to cover operating costs.

The network's community service projects, such as making maps for handicapped residents, receive financial support from Kobe city. The organization has also received grants for overhead expenses, such as office equipment, from some foundations.

According to a network representative, it is hard to keep the network going financially. Two or more paid staff who coordinate activities are required and to ensure quality, those staff should be paid properly. But it is difficult to do so under the present situation.[4]

The network obtained qualification as a specified nonprofit corporation in October 2000 in order to gain social trust.

MIYAGI ZAŌ SHIROISHI SKI RESORT   This ski resort in Miyagi prefecture opened in 1969 and, when the private company managing it went bankrupt in December 1997, ownership of the facility was transferred to the city of Shiroishi. However, city authorities lacked the funds to run it and could not find a private enterprise to manage it until a citizens' group stepped forward. The citizen's group established an NPO, Fubō Azalea, to which the city administration entrusted the management of the ski resort in 1999. In addition to running the resort, Fubō Azalea is preserving the natural environment, increasing local awareness regarding environmental protection, and working to improve skiing-related skills.

Fiscal 1999 saw a 29 percent year-on-year increase in the number of visitors to the resort. This is because the city spent ¥200 million to install another ski lift and Fubō Azalea's ski club membership increased to 330, with volunteers helping to provide skiing classes. As a result, the organization had a surplus that year of ¥20 million, which it donated to the city authorities. In fiscal 2000, the city further improved the facilities by adding a rest house.

The NPO's running of the resort has, however, come into question. First, employees' wages are much lower than when the resort was under private management, because the employees are now NPO staff. Second, the fact that the fiscal 1999 profits were donated to the city means that the resort may not be truly independent from the city administrators. Third, the city authorities' support and investment in equipment may be considered unfair by neighboring privately owned ski resorts. This is the first time that a ski resort has been managed by an NPO, but it may not be the last.

THE KUROKABE   A bank building put up in 1900 in Nagahama city, Shiga prefecture, came to be known affectionately by local citizens as the Kurokabe bank because of its black outer walls. So, when it was scheduled to be torn down, eight citizens established Kurokabe Inc. to preserve the city's heritage, encourage the practical use of historical structures, and promote activity in the city center. The city of Nagahama together with the eight volunteers financed the company's incorporation.

The enterprise currently exhibits and sells domestically made glass handicrafts; imports, exhibits, and sells overseas art glassware; manages a glass studio and sells original works made of glass; manages a restaurant; provides lessons in glass making and plans related events; and engages in international exchanges. Twenty-eight black-painted edifices are currently being operated by Kurokabe, which plans to list on the over-the-counter (OTC) market. The economic success it has experienced to date is the result of the highly skilled staff and management of this private-sector initiative, even though it is partly capitalized by the city administration. Kurokabe's fiscal 1990 sales of ¥190 million and 205,000 visitors had, by 2000, increased to sales of ¥740 million and 1,898,000 visitors.

The enterprise has also set up a town planning company to conduct similar activities in the city of Esashi, Iwate prefecture. The Nagahama city authorities opposed any investment in Esashi, so the setting up of the company caused some of the founding members closely tied to the preservation movement to resign as directors.

Nevertheless, Kurokabe Inc. has achieved great success as an enterprise and created many jobs in the community, especially for women. However, the enterprise has admittedly moved away from its original objective, to preserve the old building and original culture of the community, and is now more akin to a venture business. This underlines the difficulty in balancing social and profit goals.

## Local Support Systems in Action

For CBs to be successful, local communities must be responsive. Below are introduced two kinds of local support systems for CBs.

COMMUNITY BUSINESS SUPPORT IN HYOGO PREFECTURE    Since fiscal 1999, the Hyogo prefectural government has supported CBs in the area damaged by the Great Hanshin-Awaji Earthquake of January 1995. The area around Kobe suffered serious damage, 6,300 lives were lost, lifelines had to be set up, transportation networks rebuilt, and production equipment replaced. The amount of damage is thought to have totaled about ¥9,600 billion. Kobe, the main city in the region, had developed around the local harbor since it was first opened in 1868. Smokestack industries, such as shipbuilding and steel, sprang up early in the twentieth century and the city enjoyed a long period of prosperity, but, in recent years, the region's economy has been declining as a result of the stagnation of these industries. The damage caused by the earthquake had a negative effect on the region's economy, a situation that was aggravated as nationwide unemployment expanded. The region had an urgent need to create new jobs.

In fiscal year 2001, the local government thus decided to implement projects including (1) subsidizing enterprise start-ups and providing management consultants; (2) providing consulting services for new and existing enterprises; (3) holding consultations and seminars for CB entrepreneurs; (4) establishing and managing a support center; and (5) installing a network to perform comprehensive support services for CBs. In open competition and from among several organizations, the Social Business Support Network was selected to manage the support center from 2002.

In fiscal 2001, up to ¥4 million over two years was programmed to be given to each of eight organizations operating under the first category of government projects listed above. This money was to be used to assist with start-up costs. Organizations eligible for support are decided by a specialists committee based on the following conditions: (1) an organization's activities should meet community needs, (2) users should pay for its service, (3) its workers should receive payment, (4) it should plough profits back into the community, and (5) it should remain a business.

The support center managed by the Community Support Center Kobe opened in October 1999 to provide information for those people who wish to do something for the public good. It offers internships in NPOs, and supports those who want to float CBs.

Aside from its support for CBs, the Hyogo prefectural government has put in place a flotation advice program for venture businesses, and a management course and a course on flotation for NPOs. Table 2 briefly outlines the prefecture's support programs for venture businesses, CBs, and NPOs.

COMMUNITY BUSINESS SUPPORT—THE KINKI LABOUR BANK      In 1989, the Eitai Credit Union in Tokyo, a citizens' bank, set up a loan program patterned on the workings of Germany's Eco Bank.

Since 1995, banks with similar loan systems have been set up in several regions and include the Yamagata Shokusan Bank in Yamagata prefecture, Ikeda Bank in Osaka, and Oita prefecture's Oita Credit Union. In addition, a system has also been established whereby loans may be extended to NPOs: the Kinki Labour Bank started extending NPO enterprise-support loans (*rōkin*) in April 2000.

Under the Labor Credit Association Law, labor banks were established nationwide in the 1950s to benefit laborers. In 1998, the Kinki Labour Bank, the largest such institution, saw all seven of its associated

Table 2. Comparison of Hyogo Prefecture's Support Programs for Venture and Community Businesses and Nonprofit Organizations

| | Venture Businesses | Community Businesses | NPOs |
|---|---|---|---|
| Education and study | Kickoff seminars, support seminars for women entrepreneurs, entrepreneur training seminars, venture schools | Community business seminars | Lectures on NPOs |
| Instruction and consultation | Consulting for industrialization / venture business support and instruction projects | Consultations for potential CB entrepreneurs / consulting services for new and existing enterprises | Volunteer center |
| Human resource introduction and matching | Hyogo Venture Plaza | Information center for job seekers | Volunteer center |
| Subsidies, grants-in-aid | Business plan support projects / new industry creation programs | Supporting community business start-ups in earthquake-damaged areas | Grant for voluntary activities for community revival after earthquakes / grant for Hyogo Regional Welfare Foundation's volunteer fund |
| Loans | start-up support | | Support for NPOs in earthquake-damaged areas |
| Investment | General support system / entrepreneur support system for women Creative small-and-medium-sized-enterprise creation support system | | |

Source: Materials of Kobe Empowerment Center and Hyogo prefecture.

banks merged and, by the end of March 2001, its savings totaled ¥1.35 trillion, its outstanding balance ¥92,800 million, and its client base 9,084 organizations. The bank's latest midterm management plan states its social role as building a community welfare network in cooperation with those NPOs committed to undertaking welfare work as a main activity. In all, the bank can extend a credit line of ¥200 million, with a maximum of ¥10 million available for each project without collateral, and an unspecified amount within the limits of the collateral valuation and of the expected amount to be paid back. NPOs can obtain loans for start-up costs and operating activities.

Up until December 2001, the bank had fielded inquiries regarding the possibility of it supporting 50 possible projects, including an insurance scheme to provide care for the elderly, a group home, and a workshop for the disabled. To date, 13 of the proposed projects have received loans. The Labour Bank has its own NPO evaluation system, which studies whether their projects serve the public good, if and how much financial support they receive from governments or contributions from individuals, and how many volunteers they have. NPOs eligible for the loan meet a certain level of this evaluation system. Given that this bank is one of the few to extend loans to NPOs, the percentage of loan applications that have been approved is relatively high.[5] In addition, many institutions are seeking loans to construct facilities or stop-gap loans to tide them over until such time as promised funds are made available by government authorities.

## CONCLUSION

### The Need to Redraw Business Practices

It is necessary to differentiate NPOs, CBs, and for-profit organizations according to both the activities involved and those who benefit therefrom, rather than the ideology of the enterprises. This is especially true in the case of Japan, where the structure of the corporate system has often led for-profit organizations to set up CBs. Thus, by extension, it may be useful to rethink how a CB is defined, bearing in mind that it is the social objectives and individual programs that should take center stage, with less emphasis on an organization's corporate aspects.

That said, any consideration of CBs from the viewpoint of social policy immediately focuses on sources of financial support, for which reason it may be necessary to impose greater restraints on the profit sharing of such enterprises. This is because shareholders who are paid dividends by a company that receives financial support from the government are indirectly benefiting from government taxes.

Also in need of change is the attitude toward the flotation of venture businesses. While such flotations are much praised in Japan, the success rate is not high. With fewer new businesses being set up, emphasis on the medium-risk, medium-return model is needed. If the flotation of such middle-tier enterprises is to be encouraged, there will have to be a safety net: Entrepreneurs will require unemployment compensation and a larger job transfer market.

Since maintaining a balance between social and commercial objectives is difficult, especially as it is often hard for the social services that a CB promotes to attract adequate funding from corporations, the CB often has no choice but to seek out a profit itself. However, once an enterprise shifts gears and becomes a for-profit entity, it invariably tends to focus on profitable projects at the expense of its original social objectives.

Despite the existence of the Law to Promote Specified Nonprofit Activities, the pursuits in which an NPO may engage are limited. Since NPOs that support industry are necessary if CBs are to develop, the activities in which NPOs can become involved must be expanded. Were that to happen, NPOs could be set up like the Silicon Valley Network (SVN), which promotes industry in Silicon Valley in the United States.[6]

CBs can take any of several corporate or cooperative forms—as can be seen mainly in Europe—so it would make a great deal of sense were there an easing of the legal restrictions that apply to the structure of Japan's cooperatives, which are mainly producer and consumer oriented. The enactment in 2002 of the law qualifying certain organizations, which nature is somewhat like mutual organizations (like alumni associations, where benefits are shared among a closed membership), as corporate bodies is meaningful. But this law offers no taxation benefits to these organizations.

Commercial financial institutions will not usually extend loans to CBs, since they do not consider profitability to be a top priority and, typically, deal in services in which profits are not high. Therefore, government capital must be made available for lending to CBs.

While the CB clearly increases employment opportunities—by allowing the elderly to continue working after they have retired, enabling women to find a job, and providing employers with further work options—unless the social objectives are met and CBs receive all-round support, the only result will be that a pool of cheap labor will have been created. Particular care must thus be taken to ensure that the appropriate public policies are in place to prevent the marginalization of women and the elderly in the labor force.

The CB is very important in Japan, in that it is linked to community well-being, the flotation of companies, and the diversification of options in the workplace. Indications are that it may even provide the impetus for Japanese society to initiate much needed fundamental structural reforms.

## NOTES

1. Moreover, since neoconservatives sought strong government under both U.K. Prime Minister Thatcher and U.S. President Ronal Reagan, national defense spending increased in both countries.
2. Profits are, however, sometimes shared by such CBs as fishermen's cooperatives.
3. Author's interview with a representative of Arete on March 6, 2001.
4. Author's interview with the manager of the Nishi Suma Danran Welfare Network on March 9, 2000.
5. Author's interview with a Kinki Labour Bank official in October 2000.
6. In this respect, the law was revised in December 2002.

## BIBLIOGRAPHY

Economic Planning Agency, ed. 2000. "Kokumin seikatsu shingikai sōgō kikaku bukai chūkan hōkoku" (Interim report of the Social Policy Council synthesis planning department). <http://www5.cao.go.jp/seikatsu/2001/0409kokuseishin/main.html>.

Fasenfest, David, ed. 1993. *Community Economic Development: Policy Development in the U.S. and U.K.* New York: St. Martin's Press.

Galaway, Burt and Joe Hudson, eds. 1993. *Community Economic Development: Perspectives on Research and Policy.* Toronto, Canada: Thompson Educational Publishing, Inc.

Hayashi Yasuyoshi. 1999. "Komyuniti bizinesu no nihonteki tenkai" (Japanese deployment of community business). *Sangyō Ricchi* 9: 38.

Hosouchi Nobutaka. 1997. "21 seiki no chūshōkigyōzō wa komyuniti bizinesu ni ari" (The small business model in the 21st century will be community business). In *Komyuniti bizinesu syō ronbun* (Short theses on community business). Tokyo: Human Renaissance Institute.

Imai Yoshihiro. 1997. "Komyuniti bizinesu ni miru shimin jigyōtai hatten no kadai to hōsaku" (The subject and policy of citizen's enterprise development in community business). In *Shimin to komyuniti no atarashii kakawarikata nitsuite no kenkyū* (Research on new ways of citizen-community interaction). Kobe, Japan: 21st Century Hyogo Project Association.

Ishizuka Hideo. 1997. "Supein no shakaiteki keizai" (The social economy of Spain). In Tomizawa Kenji and Kawaguchi Kiyoshi, eds. *Hieiri kyōdō sekutā no riron to genjitsu* (Theories and the reality of the nonprofit and cooperative sectors). Tokyo: Nihon Keizai Hyōronsha.

———. 1997. "Itaria no shakaiteki keizai" (The Italian social economy). In Tomizawa Kenji and Kawaguchi Kiyoshi, eds. *Hieiri kyōdō sekutā no riron to genjitsu* (Theories and the reality of the nonprofit and cooperative sectors). Tokyo: Nihon Keizai Hyōronsha.

Kanagawa Kōji. 2000. "Kaigohoken to NPO" (Care insurance for the elderly and NPOs). In *Chiiki shakai ni okeru kōreisha shien shisutemu no arikata ni kansuru kenkyū* (Research into a community support system for the elderly). Kobe: 21st Century Hyogo Project Association.

Katō Toshiharu. 2000. *Maikuro bizinesu* (Micro business). Tokyo: Kōdansha.

Katō Yoshimasa. 1999. "Komyuniti bizinesu no tenkai to sono hyōka" (Deployment of the community business and its evaluation). *Toshimondai Kenkyū*: 51 (5).

———, ed. 2000. *Chiiki shakai wo sasaeru komyunitī bizinesu ikusei ni kansuru kokusai hikaku kenkyū* (International comparative research on fostering community businesses that support a community). Tokyo: Toyota Foundation.

Kay, Alan. 2000. "International Comparative Study on Community Business Development: Community Business Development in Scotland, U.K. and Europe." A lecture at Kansai Institute of Information Systems, 9 February.

Koyama Masato. 2000. "NPO jigyō sapōto ron to NPO kifu shisutemu no sōsetsu" (Foundation of the NPO support loan and donation system). In *Shiga no keizai to shakai*, no. 95.

MacLeod, Greg. 1997. *From Mondragon to America: Experience in Community Economic Development.* Sydney: University College of Cape Breton Press.

Machida Yōji. 2000. *Shakaiteki kigyōka* (Social entrepreneur). Tokyo: PHP Shinsho.

Matsuura Kazue. 1998. "Yume wo katachini" (Making dreams come true) in *Ōrora*, vol. 8.

Nakai Hideo. 1993. "Igirisu no kōeki katsudō to zaigen chōtatsu no dōkō" (The trend of public-benefit activity and fund raising in Britain). In Honma Masaaki, ed. *Firansoropī no shakai keizaigaku* (Social economics of philanthropy). Tokyo: Toyo Keizai Shinpōsha.

Nakajima Dai. 1998. "Shimin jigyō" (Citizen enterprise). In *Toshimondai Kenkyū* 89: 3.

Salamon, Lester M. 1995. *Partners in Public Service: Government-Nonprofit*

*Relations in the Modern Welfare State.* Baltimore, Md.: The Johns Hopkins University Press.

Shibukawa Tomoaki. 2001. *Fukushi NPO* (Welfare-oriented NPOs). Tokyo: Iwanami Shoten.

Spencer, Jerry. 2000. "Development of Community Economy in Liverpool." A lecture sponsored by Kobe Multimedia Internet Council, Kobe, Japan, 7 December.

Takekawa Shōgo. 1999a. *Fukushi shakai no shakai seisaku* (The social policy of the welfare society). Tokyo: Hōritsu Bunkasha.

———. 1999b. *Shakai seisaku no naka no gendai* (The present situation regarding social policy). Tokyo: Tokyo Daigaku Shuppankai.

Taub, Richard P. 1994. *Community Capitalism: The South Shore Bank's Strategy for Neighborhood Revitalization.* Boston, Mass.: Harvard Business School Press.

Twelvetrees, Alan C. 1996. *Organizing for Neighbourhood Development: A Comparative Study of Community Based Development Organizations.* Aldershot, U.K.: Avebury.

# 3

## Local Government and Residnt Foreigners: A Changing Relationship

### Kashiwazaki Chikako

This chapter traces the development of local government policy with regard to foreign residents. As their ethnic diversity has increased, so have their numbers; the sharp rise that commenced in the 1980s resulted at the end of 2000 in there being approximately 1.7 million registered foreigners, representing 1.3 percent of the country's population (figure 1; Japan Immigration Association 2001) But this official figure does not reflect the true ethnic diversity of Japanese society, for it includes neither the undocumented foreigners—estimated to total 230,000 as of January 1, 2001[1]  who have overstayed their visas, nor those who have their roots in another country but have acquired Japanese citizenship either through naturalization or because one parent is a Japanese national.[2]

The government needs to respond at the local-government level to this growth in ethnic diversity, because it is the municipal authorities that are primarily responsible for providing social services and administering those policies that have a direct bearing on the lives of foreign residents. In the 1990s, an increasing number of local governments

Figure 1. Number of Registered Foreigners in Japan

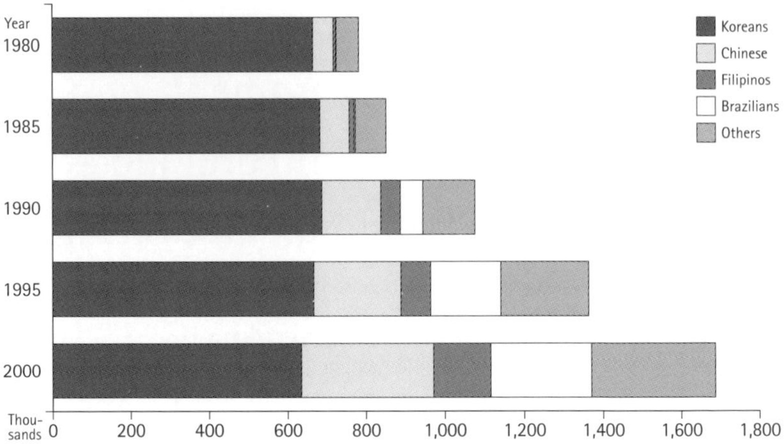

*Source:* Immigration Bureau (1993, 250); Japan Immigration Association (1996; 2001).

developed programs and policies for resident foreigners—as opposed to those who were merely tourists—and it is to these individuals that this chapter refers when discussing foreign resident programs and policies.

## FOREIGN RESIDENT POLICY: A GOVERNMENT PERSPECTIVE

There is a growing body of Japanese-language literature on local government programs and initiatives concerning resident foreigners (Ebashi 1993; Komai and Watado 1997), and research topics include partnerships between local governments and nongovernmental organizations (NGOs) (Watado 1996), as well as political participation by foreign residents (Miyajima 2000).

Though informative and useful for interlocality comparisons, the existing research is wanting regarding two central issues: the relationship between the growing concern for foreign resident policy in recent years and the earlier situation when Koreans accounted for the vast majority of the foreign resident population; and the way the concept of internationalization has been loosely linked to foreign residents.

The need to accommodate foreign residents in local communities has been interpreted as the need for Japanese society to achieve domestic internationalization—*uchinaru kokusaika* in Japanese. While there is considerable variation in the understanding of what is meant by this term, it is generally employed in reference to the interaction between Japanese and foreign nationals in Japan, rather than international exchange activities overseas (Pak 2000, 249–250).

This chapter considers the role of local-level internationalization, the broad policy framework formulated at the national level, in shaping the ways municipal governments design programs focusing on foreign residents. Such internationalization has no doubt been useful to the extent that it has provided local governments with a channel for developing foreign resident policy. It could be argued, however, that Japan's interpretation of internationalization and its subsequent application in the creation of a policy framework has had its limitations: First, it has resulted in foreign resident policy being treated as merely a derivative of international exchange projects; second, the interpretation is based on the relationship between the rigid categories of Japanese versus foreign.

## POLICY PLANS EVOLVE

### Local Government Policy on Korean Residents of Japan[3]

From the end of World War II until around 1980, most of the foreign residents in Japan were Koreans, of whom there were approximately 600,000 in 1980. A smaller group of these residents, also former colonial subjects, comprised Taiwanese.[4]

Until 1980, local governments did not consider resident foreigners to be part of the local community and administrative services were extended only to those of Japanese nationality.[5] Thus, for example, local governments would send a notice concerning the start of primary-level schooling for six-year-old children only to Japanese parents. Policies toward foreigners were administered mostly at the national level, the emphasis being on control, and resident foreigners were, first and foremost, subject to the Immigration Control and Refugee Recognition Act and the Alien Registration Law. They were denied many of the social rights due to nationality-based eligibility restrictions that existed on, for example, the national pension plan, public housing, and public-sector employment.

However, in response to demands by Korean residents of Japan, municipal governments had instituted programs to serve foreign residents in some areas, despite restrictions at the national level. Thus, by the late 1970s, the majority of municipalities had an ordinance that extended to foreign residents' national health care, which had been previously, by law, available only to Japanese citizens (Yoshioka 1995, 53–57).[6] But changes at the national level occurred only around 1980, after the Japanese government agreed to admit a small number of Indo-Chinese refugees for resettlement. Once it had joined international conventions on human rights and refugees, the Japanese government was compelled to largely abolish nationality-based eligibility restrictions in social security and housing.

## Local-Level Internationalization

In the 1980s, Japan emerged as a major economic power, and the term internationalization became a popular slogan with policymakers seeking to overcome the country's insularity. At the grass-roots level, diverse partnerships with sister cities around the world increased, as international exchange programs expanded and involved ever greater numbers of citizens (see chapter 4).

In 1987, the then-Ministry of Home Affairs (which in January 2001 incorporated other ministries and was renamed the Ministry of Public Management, Home Affairs, Posts and Telecommunications), together with the Ministries of Foreign Affairs and Education, launched the Japan Exchange and Teaching (JET) Programme. Under this program, young university graduates were invited from abroad to take part in cultural exchanges.[7] As David McConnell (2000, 39) puts it, the Ministry of Home Affairs had been one of the least international ministries and hence was an unlikely sponsor of such a project. Nevertheless, in the same year it issued guidelines for local authorities' international exchanges and embarked on a comprehensive local-level internationalization plan. The 1989 Guidelines for the Local International Exchange Promotion Plan[8] instructed prefectures and the twelve largest cities to prepare a policy package for the advancement of international exchange, and to offer financial support to new projects in that area. The development of an organizational infrastructure followed.

In 1988, the Council of Local Authorities for International Relations (CLAIR) was established and, beginning in 1989, the Ministry of Home Affairs recognized one organization per prefecture or per one of the twelve designated cities as the local international exchange association or quasi-governmental association (quango) that was to play a central role in organizing grass-roots international exchange activities. In 1995, the ministry went further and issued Guidelines for the Local International Cooperation Plan, thereby defining international cooperation as another component of the grass-roots-level internationalization plan.

At the core of the national policy of local-level internationalization was an economic goal, namely, "to revitalize localities through the creation of a community that is connected with the global society" (Nagasawa 1987, 27). To this end, local authorities were expected "to promote international exchange programs by taking advantage of each locality's unique features, raise awareness among local residents concerning international understanding, thereby establishing a local identity in the global society, and promote local industry and economy" (Nagasawa, 1987, 27). The Ministry of Home Affairs expected the exchange promotion plans to result in the following.

1. The development of local government-led international exchange programs as well as the provision of financial and other forms of support for initiatives by the private sector (setting up sister-city affiliations; organizing cultural, academic, and athletic exchanges and festivals; and developing citizens' awareness programs.)

2. The internationalization of local industries and economies, and increased tourism.

3. The creation of an environment in which local Japanese and non-Japanese residents can live together comfortably, improved administrative services would be available, and education assistance would be offered to those children who have lived and attended school abroad and required help in catching up with the local syllabus (Kaneda et al. 1993, 10–13).

Of the above points, most relevant to foreign residents are the creation of a comfortable living environment and the provision of improved administrative services, to which end the 1988 Guidelines for

the Creation of Localities for International Exchange specifically recommended the use of foreign languages on maps, signs, and in public
facilities; the publication of foreign-language guidebooks explaining
community life; and the organizing of festivals and events in which
foreigners and Japanese could take part (Chiba 1989, 39–40). Simultaneously with the issuance of these guidelines, the Ministry of Home
Affairs launched a project to promote localities that were committed
to furthering international exchange, and subsidized local government
initiatives that were in accordance with its recommendations.

It should be noted that the ministry's guidelines and recommendations reflect a perception of foreigners primarily as guests of—not residents in, and citizens of—local communities. The concept of foreign
resident policy was absent. Instead, the ministry's perception was that
international exchange—and, by extension, the revitalization of local
communities—would be facilitated simply by providing services for
foreigners. Moreover, the plight of the long-term residents originally
from Korea, Taiwan, and mainland China, many of whom had been
born and raised in Japan, received scant attention.

## Foreign Resident Population Grows

When the Ministry of Home Affairs embarked on internationalization in the mid-1980s, little attention was paid to the presence of resident foreigners. Beginning in the 1970s, the entertainment industry
absorbed many of the growing number of migrant women who were
entering Japan. They were not considered "foreign workers" (*gaikokujin rōdōsha*) as the term was generally associated with traditional blue-
collar jobs. The presence of foreign workers only came to be an issue
in the late 1980s, with the arrival of a significant number of male migrants, mainly from other Asian countries, many of whom overstayed
their visas and took jobs in the construction, manufacturing, food
processing, and other industries in which employers were finding it increasingly difficult to attract Japanese workers.[9] It was in part to stem
the increasing ranks of these undocumented workers that an amend-
ment to the immigration control law was passed in 1990. One major
consequence of the changed law was the influx of large numbers of
ethnic Japanese from South American countries, particularly Brazil.[10]

The population distribution of newly arrived foreign residents has been highly uneven, with wide local variations in terms of countries of origin and employment patterns. While Tokyo has attracted people of diverse nationalities and occupations (Machimura 2000), industrial towns and cities—such as Ōta and Ōizumi (both in Gunma prefecture), Hamamatsu, and Toyota—boast concentrations of second-generation Brazilians of Japanese descent (Yamanaka 2000, 134–135), and some rural communities—such as the Mogami area in Yamagata prefecture—have become home to a number of foreign brides, who have come to fill the needs of those farming families that have had difficulty finding Japanese women to marry farmers (Sellek 2000, 180–183). In other places, such as Osaka city, many among the foreign community are Koreans who came to Japan before the end of World War II.

## Increased Problems and Government Responses

As the ethnic composition of local communities has changed, local authorities have been forced to respond to a variety of problems—such as housing, social security, medical care, education, and human rights—that are particularly acute in those localities in which the proportion of foreign residents has grown rapidly over a short period. Public housing complexes with a high concentration of foreign residents have had their share of friction involving Japanese and foreign residents new to the area, while in the private housing market, foreign nationals seeking accommodation often face discrimination and have difficulty finding a guarantor, who would normally have to be a Japanese national. The language barrier has been evident in local schools, which have often been reluctant to accommodate children who do not speak Japanese, as well as in hospitals and the courts, where interpreters with a good knowledge of technical terms are in short supply. Furthermore, since a large number of foreign residents are not covered by health insurance, some hospitals have been reluctant to treat uninsured patients in a bid to avoid having to shoulder the high costs of emergency medical care.

Municipal responses to the above problems have included a variety of services designed to support foreign residents, including Japanese-language classes, multilingual information brochures, legal consultation services, and financial support for emergency medical care (Ebashi 1993). In order to provide services to foreign residents, some local governments have also sought to cooperate with NGOs involved in supporting resident foreigners.[11]

Meanwhile, Korean residents of Japan continued to fight against discrimination and for improved legal status. The 1981 revision of the immigration control law extended permanent-resident status to first- and second-generation Koreans who had not benefited from the permanent-resident-by-treaty status that had been introduced under the 1965 Japan-South Korea treaty. Since the national policy toward foreign residents continued to emphasize control, the 1980s saw Koreans as central players among foreign nationals opposing the legal requirement that a fingerprint be affixed to a resident's alien registration card —which every foreign resident is required by law to have in easy reach at all times for the purpose of identification. Although the Ministry of Justice was in charge of this requirement, it was at municipal government offices that foreign residents reported to have their fingerprints taken, and some of these authorities took a more liberal view of the regulation and refrained from reporting dissidents to national administrative offices.

In the 1990s, Koreans were active in campaigning for the right to public-sector employment, participation in local elections, ethnic education, and social security. As a result, in 2000 several groups of Diet members submitted different versions of bills to give local voting rights to permanent resident foreigners.

A major issue in the area of education has been ethnic schooling. Excluded from the categories of ordinary educational institutions, Korean schools are disadvantaged in that, for example, their students are not eligible to apply for entry into national universities. Meanwhile, only a limited number of public schools offer programs designed to foster ethnic identity among students of Korean descent.

Furthermore, despite the principle of equality between Japanese nationals and foreigners in the area of social security, when, in the 1980s, the government abolished the nationality requirement for the national pension scheme, no transitional measures were introduced, as a result of which elderly foreign residents who had earlier been denied the opportunity to join the scheme still found themselves left with no old-age pension. In a bid to remedy the situation, a number of local governments have in recent years provided these elderly residents with special welfare allowances.

The language barrier is a major problem for those who have recently arrived in Japan, and their needs tend to differ somewhat from those of long-term residents whose settlement originated in the colonial era. However, both groups share the same goal of securing basic rights as local residents and participating fully in their local communities. Parallel with the demands from both the newer and the better-established foreign residents, the scope of foreign resident–related policy expanded from merely providing information and services to facilitating foreign-resident participation in local administration. Several local governments have launched councils for resident foreigners, such as the Kawasaki City Representative Assembly for Foreign Residents, set up in 1996. Other measures to facilitate political participation include the appointment by local authorities of foreign citizens as advisory committee members or citizen monitors.

The legal and administrative functions of municipalities are, however, limited and broader responsibilities are borne at the national level. Thus, the Ministry of Health, Labor and Welfare is in charge of social security and medical care; the Ministry of Education, Culture, Sports, Science and Technology oversees Japanese-language teaching and ethnic education in schools; and the Ministry of Justice controls immigration and visa status. The central government, further, has maintained that in connection with public-sector employment, foreign nationals are not allowed "to exercise public authority or to take part in the formation of a public will" (Okazaki 1998, 13–14). Originally formulated by the Cabinet Legislation Bureau in 1953, this official stance has been repeatedly invoked to limit the trend to liberalize nationality requirements for public administration positions.

The problems faced by resident foreigners do not fall neatly into the international exchange category, as they have been classified by the national government, and cannot be solved by the local government initiatives that adhere to the Ministry of Home Affairs' project to promote localities committed to furthering international exchange. For, whereas such projects might incidentally benefit foreign nationals settled in local communities, the main purpose for which they were organized was to facilitate exchange activities with foreigners who come to Japan either just to visit or to stay for a short time. Local-level internationalization devised at the national level thus has failed to address the problems of resident foreigners.

## FOREIGN-RESIDENT POLICY FORMULATION BEGINS

In the 1990s, some local government authorities took the initiative and developed—as had a few in the previous decade—foreign resident–related policies despite national-level legal and administrative restrictions. Four approaches to this policy formulation are cited below. Although the administrative units in these examples differ in size and government level—in that two are bed towns, another is one of the twelve large cities designated by law, and the fourth is a prefecture—all four have accommodated foreign nationals as residents since before the introduction of the Ministry of Home Affairs' internationalization plan.

### Takatsuki City

Located between the cities of Osaka and Kyoto, Takatsuki has a population of approximately 360,000. During World War II, conscripted Korean laborers were brought to the area to build factories and, after the war, a Korean district formed. At present, Koreans represent about two-thirds of the city's 2,900 foreign residents, who account for 0.8 percent of the population (Takatsuki City 1982).

Two factors explain why Takatsuki has been a leader in developing foreign-resident policy despite its relatively small number of foreign residents. One is the city's history of interaction with the Korean community. Since the 1970s, a local Korean group known as Mukuge no Kai has been demanding that the city improve the status of those residents of Korean descent, and its negotiations with the city have contributed to the step-by-step abolition of the nationality requirement for positions in local government offices as well as to the development of educational projects for Korean children.

The second factor is the city's emphasis on the protection of human rights. In 1978, the city declared that it would uphold the principles of human rights, ahead of the central government's ratification, the following year, of international conventions on human rights. Its responsibility to serve the Korean community was interpreted by the city as part of its overall duty to protect human rights and raise public awareness regarding the concerns of minorities.

But Takatsuki's approach is, perhaps, best illustrated in the area of education. In 1979, the city issued the Basic Policy Concerning the Problems of Residents of Korean Descent. The city thus placed the education of Korean children under the rubric of human rights education, thereby relating it to the problems faced by the *buraku* people, a caste-like minority long subject to discrimination by the majority Japanese, as well as the physically and mentally challenged. In 1985, the city launched an education project for Koreans that included on the steering committee representatives from Korean organizations. Among the programs were a children's program, a junior high school program, Japanese-language classes, and social events to raise the level of public awareness regarding issues pertaining to the Korean minority population.

While this municipal education project was initially focused on Korean residents, it has now been adapted to meet the needs of other newcomers, including the children of so-called Chinese returnees—those Japanese who were left behind in China, during the times of political confusion during and at the end of World War II, and their immediate relatives—and Filipino children. While the city has appointed instructors at public schools to assist those students in need of Japanese-language lessons, municipal programs targeting newcomers are still in their infancy.

Three departments at the Takatsuki city office are involved in foreign resident policy: the Human Rights Promotion Division, the Board of Education, and the Exchange Program Division. The focus of the Exchange Program Division is on such conventional international exchanges as sister-city programs, although it also offers Japanese-language classes for foreign residents. Likewise, the Takatsuki International Association, which is mainly engaged in international exchange programs, also has a link for residents, to whom it offers consultation services. Overall, the city's foreign-resident policy has not been entirely subsumed in international programs, in contrast to the situation in other cities, where an office in charge of international exchange may well simultaneously cover programs for foreign residents.

Moreover, in Takatsuki, programs for Koreans who have resided in the country for some time still remain quite separate from those for foreign nationals who have arrived more recently, perhaps reflecting the early institutionalization of certain Korean resident–related programs and the fact that there is only a relatively small number of newcomer foreign nationals in the city. Although the city plans to adopt a comprehensive internationalization scheme by merging its international exchange and foreign resident policies, that might be quite a challenge, because the former has emphasized "outward" exchange programs whereas the latter has focused on the rights of resident Koreans.

### Toyonaka City

Located northwest of Osaka, this city has some 4,800 resident foreigners who account for 1.2 percent of its 390,000 residents.[12] While Koreans comprise the majority of these foreigners, an increasing number of recent arrivals from China are settling in the city. Like Takatsuki, Toyonaka has been responsive to its foreign resident population and so, for example, abolished the nationality requirement for all jobs in municipal offices in 1981, the year when Japan joined the refugee convention. In the area of ethnic education, the city has a Basic Educational Policy for Resident Foreigners, according to which budgetary allocations are made for such programs as summer schooling for the children of Korean residents of Japan.

Also like Takatsuki, Toyonaka initially approached issues concerning Koreans primarily from a human rights perspective but, unlike Takatsuki, in the 1990s it developed a comprehensive policy to promote grass-roots internationalization. This involved heeding the concerns of long-time and newly arrived Korean residents, and integrating the city's international exchange and foreign-resident policies.

An effort to formulate internationalization programs began in 1989, partly in response to the 1987 guidance issued by the Ministry of Home Affairs.[13] In 1991, the section in charge of international exchange was moved under control of the newly inaugurated Human Rights and Cultural Affairs Department, and now the section has become the Cultural and International Affairs Section, which currently coordinates the overall internationalization plan that includes foreign residents–related programs.

In 2000, the city announced the Basic Guidelines for Promoting Internationalization: living together and working together for local-level internationalization. The document clearly defines foreign residents as citizens, and internationalization as involving protecting their human rights, providing them with social services, recognizing them as cocitizens with the Japanese, and accepting them as residents in the community (Toyonaka City 2000, 21). This understanding of internationalization is considerably different from that of the Ministry of Home Affairs.

The above-mentioned basic guidelines are designed to ensure: (1) the protection of human rights and the promotion of cross-national understanding; (2) internationalization of school education, including assistance for newcomer children, programs to foster ethnic identity among students of Korean descent, and the development of a curriculum for intercultural understanding; (3) the development of a foreign-resident policy; (4) internationalization of the city's administration, including assistance for foreign residents through information and consultation services, political participation by foreign residents, and human resource development for facilitating internationalization programs; (5) promotion of international exchange and cooperation; and (6) citizens' participation in the aforementioned programs.

The Toyonaka Association for Intercultural Activities and Communication plays a major role in implementing the above policy and strives to encourage its citizens to take the initiative in international exchanges and create a community in which Japanese and foreign citizens live together, and also endeavors to persuade all citizens to work together for the common good. The association is active in international exchange activities overseas and programs concerning foreign residents. In addition to consultation services for newly arrived foreign residents, it also offers such programs for long-time residents as a monthly gathering for the children of long-term Korean residents, and helps them learn about their Korean heritage.

Toyonaka's comprehensive plan for internationalization and its emphasis on foreign-resident policies is the result of three main factors. First, since its programs for long-term Korean residents were not as institutionalized as those of Takatsuki, it was probably easier to place them under the heading of internationalization. Second, the city's 1996 master plan linked both the human rights concerns of Korean residents and the promotion of international exchanges to the goal of "creating a peaceful and egalitarian society" (Toyonaka City 2000, 14). Third, both scholars from among the city's Korean residents and NPO representatives active in promoting a multicultural community were members of the city's internationalization policy committee, and were probably instrumental in making foreign resident–related issues central to the guidelines.

When it comes to policy implementation, however, it is still early days. As evidence of the internationalization of the city's administration, for instance, there was still no more than a Japanese-language version of the city's newsletter in 2000, although preparation for a multilingual publication was under way. But there was progress in other areas; Japanese-language lessons for foreign children and interpreting services began in schools in 1998. And plans are also afoot to establish an organ for foreign citizens' participation in local governance to fulfill the city's goal of promoting citizen participation.

### The City of Osaka

Osaka, the major city in western Japan and the center of trade and commerce, is home to the largest community of Korean residents of Japan. Of the city's population of 2.6 million, foreign residents account for about 4.6 percent, the highest proportion among Japan's twelve largest cities (Japan Immigration Association 2000). The number of Koreans, who account for over 80 percent of Osaka's foreign residents, is declining, but new arrivals from other countries are gradually increasing.

Osaka is characterized by both its relationship with the Korean community, and its desire to become international. Historically, Koreans have experienced major political struggles in Osaka, particularly in the area of education. In the years following Japan's defeat in World War II, Koreans demanded the right to a Korean education within the public school system, but the Japanese authorities made few concessions.[14] Yet the Korean community and teacher organizations persisted, organizing special classes outside the ordinary school curriculum to foster Korean children's awareness of their ethnic identity. As a result, Osaka has, since 1992, appropriated a budget for these classes, which have been steadily increasing in number.[15] As in the case of Takatsuki, Osaka's interaction with its Korean community has made it responsive to the concerns of the overall foreign-resident population.

Osaka's desire to become international is well served by its extensive overseas connections. The opening of the Kansai International Airport in 1994 increased the city's ability to welcome visitors from abroad, and each year it hosts a number of international events. Thus, for example, the city has made it a point to ensure that signs of importance in public places are written in roman script as well as Japanese characters.

As one of Japan's main cities, Osaka was asked by the Ministry of Home Affairs to draw up a master plan for internationalization, which it did in 1997. The Basic Directives for the Promotion of Internationalization in Osaka is based on the principles of international exchange; international cooperation; attracting visitors from abroad (*shūkyaku*); and accommodating residents from abroad (*kyōsei*). Osaka's perception of internationalization emphasizes establishing overseas links, and its connection to foreign-resident policy seems weak.

The detached nature of Osaka's foreign-resident policy is reflected in the city's internal structure. The Human Rights Division coordinates foreign-resident policy, whereas the International Relations Department of the mayor's office is in charge of the broader internationalization plan. The organizational features of Osaka are, therefore, more similar to those of Takatsuki than of Toyonaka. However, Osaka does not have separate policies for long-term and newly arrived residents, while its foreign-resident policy is relatively autonomous and independent within the internationalization policy framework.

In 1998, Osaka city's Human Rights Department compiled and published the Basic Guidelines for Foreign Resident Policy, the main objectives of which are the protection of the human rights of foreign residents, the formation of a multicultural society, and enabling foreign residents to take part in public life. The document outlines the current situation and elaborates on the policy requirements in areas such as administrative services, education, mutual understanding, and local community participation. It is a comprehensive policy plan that pays attention to both long-term Korean residents and newly arrived people of other nationalities. In the area of education, the guidelines specifically mention the need to give special consideration to those children who are naturalized or have dual nationality (Osaka City 1998, 18–19). This is particularly noteworthy, since the framework of internationalization or foreign-resident policy does not automatically cover children who have their roots abroad but have Japanese nationality. To be sure, schools pay attention to the problems of children whose native language is not Japanese, regardless of nationality status. However, those without linguistic barriers are generally treated as "Japanese," that is, little effort is made to recognize and foster their "ethnic" identity. Osaka has also encouraged foreign residents to participate in the policymaking process, as a result of which well-informed foreign citizens participate in the foreign-resident policy committee, a few being members of the city's various deliberation committees.[16]

International House, Osaka, was set up in 1987 and has been designated the Local International Exchange Association. As in Toyonaka, it organizes a good part of the city's internationalization-related programs, including an information service for foreign residents. An Information Center offers a multilingual consultation service for resident foreigners staffed by regular members and volunteers, and is equipped for teleconferencing to facilitate consultations.[17] As foreign residents have come to stay longer in Japan in recent years, it has become increasingly likely that they will consult the center on such issues vital to their day-to-day living as health care coverage and childbirth.[18] While the International House is thus active in serving newly arrived foreign residents, there are few programs designed for long-term Korean residents.

### Kanagawa Prefecture

Kanagawa, a prefecture adjacent to Tokyo, has a population of 8.5 million and as of the end of 2000, the foreign-resident population was approximately 120,000, or 1.4 percent of the prefecture's population (Japan Immigration Association 2001). The prefecture's two major cities are Yokohama and Kawasaki, the latter having a well-established Korean community and active Korean citizens' organizations. While Korean residents have been decreasing in number and now represent somewhat less than 30 percent of the prefecture's foreign-resident population, there has been a marked increase in the number of new resident foreigners since the 1980s, including Chinese (22 percent of the foreign-resident population), Brazilians (10 percent), and Filipinos (10 percent). In addition, more than 5,000 Indo-Chinese refugees —Vietnamese, Cambodians, and Laotians—reside in the prefecture, their concentration here being due to there having been a national center for the settlement of Indo-Chinese refugees in Yamato city between 1980 and 1998.

Kanagawa's active involvement in international exchange projects preceded the central government's initiative by many years. Elected in 1975, former Governor Nagasu Kazuji was an advocate of people-to-people diplomacy (*minsai gaikō*), and encouraged grass-roots cross-national exchanges and cooperation in the interests of peace and for the common good. Applying the concept of diplomacy at the local government level or to activities conducted by ordinary citizens was a novel idea at the time,[19] but soon the appropriate organizational infrastructure was developed, with the setting up of the International Exchange Section in the prefecture's Public Relations Department in 1976, and the establishment of the Kanagawa International Association in 1977.

While these people-to-people diplomacy programs involved overseas friendship exchanges such as sister-city affiliations, they also came to be applied at the local level reflecting the need to accommodate foreign residents in the local community. The first major effort by Kanagawa prefecture to tackle the issue of foreigners as residents took the form of a research project conducted in 1982 and sponsored by its local governance research center. A team of officials conducted interviews with foreign residents of Korean descent living in the prefecture and the report subsequently compiled by the research team provided the incentive for the prefecture to conduct a broader survey of long-term foreign residents in 1984. Since the Indo-Chinese refugees were at around this time swelling the newly arrived resident population, the foreign-resident policy that was drawn up by the local authorities was designed to cater for the needs of both long-term and newly arrived residents.

As has been the case in Osaka, the policy package for foreign residents in Kanagawa is considered a part of the broader international policy. The latest master plan, issued in 2000, is entitled the New Kanagawa International Policy Promotion Plan, revised. It features foreign-resident policy as one of the main areas of international policy with the slogan, "Building a regional community for coexistence with foreign residents," and stresses the concept of participation by foreign citizens in both the prefectural government and community life. In order to facilitate participation, the plan urges that human rights be protected, multilingual information be made available, greater efforts be made to provide administrative services, and that support be given to those seeking accommodation.[20]

Kanagawa has been among the leaders in implementing foreign resident–related policies. In 1998, the prefecture launched the Kanagawa Foreign Residents' Council as an advisory body to the governor, with the stipulation that its policy recommendations are to be incorporated in the formulation of international policy. On the whole, conditions in the prefecture have been conducive to the development of foreign-resident policy, the people-to-people diplomacy under the reformist governor having led to the accumulation of grass-roots-level expertise in citizens' organizations, the International Association having played a major role in facilitating networking among NGOs.

In each of the four cases discussed above, there is common recognition that local government needs to have a systematic foreign-resident policy, that the Ministry of Home Affairs' local-level internationalization program has helped shape local policy structure, and that there is growing emphasis on the concept of participation, based on the recognition that the provision of services is necessary but not sufficient if foreign residents are to be treated as citizens and members of the community.

## THE EFFECTIVENESS AND LIMITATIONS OF DOMESTIC INTERNATIONALIZATION

Advocating internationalization has helped start to ease open Japan's closed society, while advocating domestic internationalization has contributed to raising public awareness regarding the problems faced by foreign residents. Nevertheless, there are two major problems with using internationalization as the umbrella under which to develop policies to respond to Japan's increasing ethnic diversity.

First, international exchange and cooperation are the main focuses of internationalization policy, and foreign-resident policy tends to be treated only as a side issue without autonomous status. To be sure, some local governments, such as those of Toyonaka, Osaka, and Kanagawa, have developed innovative foreign resident–related plans, even under the rubric of internationalization and often by taking advantage of the appeal this concept has in Japan.[21] Takatsuki city has the potential to develop a more comprehensive foreign-resident policy by building on its experience in working with the Korean community, while some other local governments that experienced an influx of new arrivals in the 1990s have made efforts to respond effectively to the concerns of foreign residents.

The same cannot be expected of a great number of other localities, however. Following the administrative guidance of the central government, all prefectures and the country's twelve largest cities drew up plans for the promotion of local-level internationalization, mostly following the suggestions of the Ministry of Home Affairs (Iwata 1994). While the model designed at the national level did bring some concrete benefits—the popularization of guidebooks for foreign residents—internationalization as a slogan can shift the focus away from such central tasks of foreign-resident policy as ensuring basic civil and social rights, and facilitating participation in local society. The full development of foreign-resident policy may, therefore, be difficult when it is appended to international exchange programs.

The Ministry of Home Affairs, rather belatedly, began to pay attention to the issues of foreign residents in response to the unexpected increase in the number of foreign workers and their families. In 1992, the project to promote localities that were committed to furthering international exchange added a new category, namely, "measures for resident foreigners." In the initial year, the project allocated subsidies to Hamamatsu city (Shizuoka prefecture), Sano city (Tochigi prefecture), and Aikawa town (Kanagawa prefecture), all of which had experienced a sharp growth in the number of Brazilians and Peruvians of Japanese descent (Furukawa 1993, 28–29).

In 1998, CLAIR began a new financial-support program by merging one existing program administered by the organization and another by the Ministry of Home Affairs. Several proposals and initiatives for foreign residents have received subsidies under the new support program. Nevertheless, the Home Affairs Ministry continues to believe that providing services for foreign residents is just one aspect of internationalization.[22]

The second major problem with developing policies under the umbrella of internationalization lies in the concept itself, which assumes that exchanges take place between Japanese and foreigners and that Japanese culture is to interact with foreign culture. For the purposes of this discussion, the Japanese people and their culture are considered homogeneous, but, by insisting on the notion of homogeneous Japanese and ignoring the presence of Japanese citizens of overseas origin, the perspective on diversity is undercut. If the goal of foreign-resident policy is to develop a multicultural society, using the phrase "foreign resident" can have an adverse effect by reinforcing the rigid categorization based on nationality status. For instance, an increasing number of schools have attempted to tackle the problems faced by foreign children. However, it is often not easy to identify children with an immigrant background when they hold Japanese citizenship.

Thus there is also a need to consider whether the current programs to foster cross-national understanding are satisfactory in fostering diverse ethnic identity, and whether what would be preferable might not be "multicultural understanding" (on the basis that both Japanese and foreign citizens have diverse origins and cultural backgrounds), rather than "cross-national understanding" (on the basis of learning about foreign cultures by getting to know foreign nationals).

The challenge for local governments is twofold. First, it is necessary to formulate a comprehensive foreign-resident policy focusing on participation in local communities and on the overall social support necessary to that end. Seen from this perspective, foreign-resident policy should overlap with programs concerned with human rights protection. Second, in anticipation of the continued increase in the number of Japanese citizens of overseas origin, programs are needed to acknowledge and promote cultural diversity. Greater emphasis should be given to *tabunka kyōsei* (living together in a multicultural community) rather than internationalization. Of particular importance is multicultural education, as well as projects that encourage and support activities by a variety of cultural communities. National-level legal and financial support is vital in pursuing both these directions.

## CONCLUDING REMARKS

This chapter has examined the relevance to foreign-resident policy of local-level internationalization. In so doing, it has addressed the problems; offering solutions remains the task of others. As has been pointed out, the national-level policy framework has not always been decisive in shaping local-level outcomes. To wit the case studies above, in which the local authorities have, at times, shown some originality in formulating their policies.

While the effectiveness of programs is better judged by the measures implemented than by a mere analysis of program frameworks, the latter are, nevertheless, important. A policy framework indicates basic principles and ideals, gives direction to the organization of specific programs, and provides a basis for the ordering of priorities. And within it, some issues are emphasized while others may be left out entirely.

The term internationalization gained currency in the 1980s and, together with globalization, is still commonly used in Japan to indicate the direction in which it is hoped society shall move. In local governance, waving the banner of internationalization has the double advantage of securing financial support from the central government and the approval of the populace. Calls for internationalization have without a doubt contributed significantly to the promotion of policies regarding foreign citizens. Ironically, it is because the majority of Korean residents of Japan have maintained their nationality and not become Japanese citizens that the framework of internationalization has been accepted with ease. This, in turn, has made it possible to integrate issues pertaining to long-term and newly arrived residents.

With an increasing number of long-term Korean residents of Japan holding Japanese citizenship, the foreign-resident policy in the future needs to take into account a demographic cycle in which a percentage of foreign nationals become naturalized Japanese, while newly arrived foreigners add to the population of foreign nationals. Clearly it is time that local government policy recognize the diversity of both the Japanese and foreign nationals who reside in Japan.

The ultimate goal of the local-level internationalization plan is the revitalization of localities and, hence, importance is attached to international projects that yield economic gains for the community.

However, as residents are the local community's most valuable assets, assisting citizens of migrant origins to participate fully in public life can be an effective way of revitalizing localities.

## NOTES

1. "The number of illegally-remaining foreigners, as of January 1, 2001," Ministry of Justice, Press Release, April 2001.

2. In 1985, the Japanese nationality law adopted the principle of bilineal *jus sanguinis*: A child acquires Japanese nationality by birth if at least one parent is Japanese. For many Japanese, however, it is difficult to comprehend that a person who looks non-Japanese may be Japanese by virtue of having Japanese nationality, or that a person who looks Japanese may have non-Japanese parentage and yet have Japanese nationality, as is the case with those individuals of Korean descent. The rapid increase in international marriages is challenging the hitherto entrenched equation that citizenship = nationality = ethnicity. Nevertheless, the common assumption remains that foreign registration statistics measure the degree of ethnic diversity in society.

3. The Korean residents of Japan—known as *zainichi* Koreans (*zainichi* literally means "residing in Japan")—are mainly those individuals whose settlement in Japan originated during Japan's colonization of the Korean peninsula, although early post-1945 immigrants are also included.

4. During the colonial period, both Koreans and Taiwanese in Japan held Japanese nationality and were considered Japanese imperial subjects. When the San Francisco Peace Treaty went into effect in 1952, the Japanese government declared that all former colonial subjects, including those residing in Japan, were to be stripped of their Japanese nationality. Consequently, many of the Koreans in Japan have lived as foreign nationals since then, although the rate of naturalization has increased over the years. For background, see Kashiwazaki (2000a; 2000b).

5. The records of foreign residents are entered into the foreigners' registration system and are not combined with the Japanese household registries. In recent years, some local authorities have compiled household records by incorporating the two systems so as to provide more efficient public services.

6. However, this restriction did not apply to South Korean nationals who held permanent-resident-by-treaty status under the 1965 Japan–South Korea normalization treaty. This caused disparity among Korean residents, since those who opted not to register as South Korean—due to their support for North Korea or for some other reason—found themselves at a disadvantage. The latter group obtained permanent-resident status in 1981, as mentioned below.

7. The role of participants in the JET Programme was primarily that of

English teacher in the public school system, but the scope of the program subsequently expanded to include other activities. Since 1987, more than 25,000 people from 39 countries have taken part in the program <http://www.clair .nippon-net.ne.jp/HTML_E/JET/JET.HTM>. See McConnell (2000) on the development of the program as well as its implementation.

8. For the content of the Guidelines for the Local International Exchange Promotion Plan, see Kaneda et al. (1993, 10–13).

9. See Mori (1997) concerning Japanese labor market conditions and the growth of migration to Japan.

10. The 1990 change in the law allowed ethnic Japanese to obtain visas with no employment restrictions attached. The number of Brazilian nationals in Japan increased from 56,000 in 1990 to 176,000 in 1995 (Japan Immigration Association 1996). See also Sellek (2000, 72–84).

11. While local governments were slow to respond to the growing numbers of newly arrived foreign residents, NGOs played a major supporting role (Roberts 2000).

12. "Trend in foreign registration" (http://www.city.toyonaka.osaka.jp/ toyonaka/tokei/gif-data/980002.gif).

13. Based on the author's interview with a Toyonaka city official, November 13, 2000.

14. A well-known example is the large-scale protest movement against the closure of Korean schools in 1948, known as the Hanshin Education Struggle, which was met with a crackdown by the authorities. At that time, the Supreme Commander for the Allied Powers (SCAP) was increasingly concerned about Korean political activity and supported the severe measures taken by the Japanese government.

15. As of December 2000, 42 primary schools and 38 junior high schools were conducting special classes for the benefit of children of Korean descent (based on an interview by the author of an Osaka city official.). On the history of such special classes in Osaka, see Suzuki (1997).

16. As is the case for Toyonaka, Osaka's committee of informed citizens on foreign resident policy issued a detailed report and recommendations, which is thought to have been instrumental in enriching the 1998 Basic Guidelines for Foreign Resident Policy.

17. Currently, the center offers information in seven languages—English, Chinese, Korean, Spanish, Portuguese, Thai, and Indonesian.

18. Based on materials compiled by the International House, Osaka.

19. For the concept of *minsai gaikō* and its development, see Suzuki et al. (1990) and Kanagawa prefecture (1995).

20. In April 2001, Kanagawa prefecture launched a housing support program for foreigners, according to which volunteer staff at the newly established Housing Support Center mediate between foreign residents and real estate agencies.

21. This assessment agrees with Pak's contention that local governments in Japan have created innovative programs to incorporate foreigners into the community by redefining the national government project for local internationalization (2000, 245–46).While recognizing that local governments have a degree of autonomy from the national government, this chapter emphasizes the constraints of the national policy framework.

22. In April 2000, the Ministry of Home Affairs issued an administrative circular instructing local governments to recognize NGOs and other citizens' organizations as central players in both international exchange and international cooperation, and to assist in their activities. However, there is no mention of foreign residents, indicating that anything related to them remains subsumed in the concept of international exchange.

## BIBLIOGRAPHY

Chiba Yoshihiro. 1989. "Kokusaika shakai ni okeru chihōgyōsei no arikata ni kansuru chōsa kenkyū" (A survey on the role of local governance in the globalizing society). *Chihōjichi*, no. 498: 25–41.

Ebashi Takashi, ed. 1993. *Gaikokujin wa jūmin desu* (Foreigners are residents). Tokyo: Gakuyō Shobō.

Furukawa Tomoyuki. 1993. "'Kokusai kōryū no machi suishin purojekuto' ni tsuite." (About the project to promote localities that are committed to furthering international exchange). *Chihōjichi*, no. 543: 27–34.

Immigration Bureau. 1993. *Shutsunyūkoku kanri* (Immigration control). Tokyo: Ministry of Justice.

Iwata Katsuo. 1994. *Shin chiiki kokusaikaron* (A new theory of local-level internationalization). Kyoto: Hōritsu Bunkasha.

Japan Immigration Association. 1996. *Zairyū gaikokujin tōkei.* (Statistics on registered foreigners). Tokyo: Japan Immigration Association.

————. 2000. *Zairyū gaikokujin tōkei* (Statistics on registered foreigners). Tokyo: Japan Immigration Association.

————. 2001. *Zairyū gaikokujin tōkei* (Statistics on registered foreigners). Tokyo: Japan Immigration Association.

Kanagawa prefecture. 1995. *Minsaigaikō nijyūnen* (Twenty years of people-to-people diplomacy). Kanagawa: Kanagawa prefecture.

————. 2000. *Kaitei shin Kanagawa kokusaiseisaku suishin puran* (The new Kanagawa international policy promotion plan). Kanagawa: Kanagawa prefecture.

Kaneda Masashi, et al. 1993. *Kokusaika jidai no machizukuri* (City planning in the age of internationalization). Tokyo: Chūō Keizaisha.

Kashiwazaki, Chikako. 2000a. "Politics of Legal Status: The Equation of

Nationality with Ethnonational Identity." In Sonia Ryang, ed. *Koreans in Japan: Critical Voices from the Margin.* London: Routledge.

—. 2000b. "Citizenship in Japan: Legal Practice and Contemporary Development." In T. Alexander Aleinikoff and Douglas Klusmeyer, eds. *From Migrants to Citizens: Membership in a Changing World.* Washington, D.C.: Brookings Institution Press.

Komai Hiroshi and Watado Ichirō, eds. 1997. *Jichitai no gaikokujin seisaku* (Foreign resident policy of local governments). Tokyo: Akashi Shoten.

Machimura Takashi. 2000. "Local Settlement Patterns of Foreign Workers in Greater Tokyo: Growing Diversity and Its Consequences." In Mike Douglas and Glenda S. Roberts eds. *Japan and Global Migration.* London and New York: Routledge.

McConnell, David L. 2000. *Importing Diversity: Inside Japan's JET Programme.* Berkeley: University of California Press.

Miyajima Takashi, ed. 2000. *Gaikokujin shimin to seijisanka* (Foreign citizens and political participation). Tokyo: Yūshindō.

Mori Hiromi. 1997. *Immigration Policy and Foreign Workers in Japan.* Basingstoke, U.K.: Macmillan.

Nagasawa Jun'ichi. 1987. "Kokusaika jidai to chihōkōkyōdantai no taiō" (Local government response to the age of internationalization). *Chihōjichi,* no. 477: 22–35.

Okazaki Katsuhiko. 1998. *Gaikokujin no kōmu shūninken* (The rights of foreign nationals to occupy positions in public administration). Tokyo: Chihōjichi Sōgōkenkyūjo.

Osaka City. 1997. *Osakashi kokusaika shisaku suishin kihon shishin* (Osaka City's basic guidelines for promoting internationalization). Osaka: Osaka City.

—. 1998. *Osakashi gaikokuseki jūmin shisaku kihon shishin* (Osaka city's basic guidelines for foreign-resident policy). Osaka: Osaka City.

Pak, Katherine Tegtmeyer. 2000. "Foreigners Are Local Citizens too: Local Governments Respond to International Migration in Japan." in Mike Douglas and Glenda S. Roberts, eds. *Japan and Global Migration.* London and New York: Routledge.

Roberts, Glenda S. 2000. "NGO Support for Migrant Labor in Japan." In Mike Douglas and Glenda S. Roberts, eds. *Japan and Global Migration.* London and New York: Routledge.

Sellek, Yoko. 2000. *Migrant Labour in Japan.* Houndmills, Hampshire, U.K. and New York: Palgrave.

Suzuki Kumiko. 1997. "Osakashi: 'Zainichi' komyunitī wo naihō suru toshi" (Osaka: A city with a community of residents of Korean descent). In Komai Hiroshi and Watado Ichirō, eds. 1997. *Jichitai no gaikokujin seisaku* (Foreign resident policy of local governments). Tokyo: Akashi Shoten.

Suzuki Yūji et al. 1990. *Minsaigaikō no chōsen: Chiiki kara chikushakai e* (The struggle of people-to-people diplomacy: From locality to global society). Tokyo: Nihon Hyōronsha.

Takatsuki City. 1982. *Zainichi kankoku chōsenjin mondai torikumi ni tsuiteno kyōiku kihon hōshin* (Basic education policy concerning the problems of residents of Korean descent). Takatsuki: Takatsuki City.

Toyonaka City. 2000. *Toyonakashi kokusaika shisaku suishin kihon hōshin* (Toyonaka city basic guidelines for promoting internationalization). Toyonaka: Toyonaka City.

Watado Ichirō, ed. 1996. *Jichitai seisaku no tenkai to NGO* (Development of local government policy and its relation to NGOs). Tokyo: Akashi Shoten.

Yamanaka Keiko. 2000. "'I will go home, but when?' Labor Migration and Circular Diaspora Formation by Japanese Brazilians in Japan." In Mike Douglas and Glenda S. Roberts, eds. *Japan and Global Migration*. London and New York: Routledge.

Yoshioka Masuo. 1995. *Zainichi gaikokujin to shakaihoshō* (Resident foreigners and social security). Tokyo: Shakai Hyōronsha.

# 4 International Policies of Local Governments

## Menju Toshihiro

Local authorities in Japan have been promoting international activities since the end of World War II. According to the Ministry of Public Management, Home Affairs, Posts and Telecommunications, in fiscal year 2000 prefectural and municipal authorities set aside some ¥104.4 billion for overseas-related activities, excluding the construction of facilities. The figure was almost double what it had been a decade earlier.

Local government authorities have traditionally encouraged sister affiliations and, as of April 1, 2001, approximately a quarter of these authorities—930 in all—had set up 1,407 sister affiliations overseas (table 1).

The central government, too, has played an important role in advancing international activities at the local level. In 1989, the then-Ministry of Home Affairs[1] issued a directive, Guidance for the Promotion of Regional International Exchange, to prefectures and twelve "designated cities" (those with a population of roughly one million) asking them to take a more systematic approach to international activities

**Table 1.** Sister Affiliations (as of April 1, 2001)

|  | Prefec-ture | Cities | Special Wards | Towns | Villages | Total |
|---|---|---|---|---|---|---|
| Local governments with sister affiliations | 39 | 430 | 19 | 370 | 72 | 930 |
| Local governments with multiple affiliations | 30 | 205 | 8 | 49 | 6 | 298 |
| Total affiliations | 114 | 788 | 27 | 379 | 66 | 1,407 |

*Source:* Council of Local Authorities for International Relations (2001).

by drafting their own policy-related strategies. It also urged them to establish local international exchange associations[2] or quasi-governmental associations (quangos) to promote grass-roots international activities. As a result, as of June 2001 as many as 972 such associations had been set up by prefectures, designated cities, as well as small and

**Figure 1.** Expenditure on Internationally Related Activities by Local Governments (million yen)

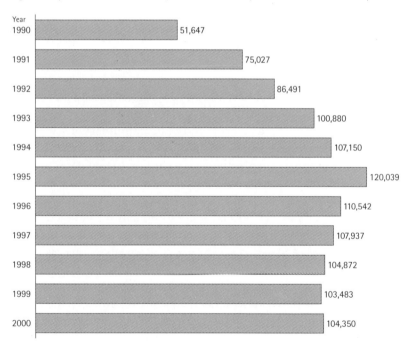

*Source:* Internal documents of the Ministry of Public Management, Home Affairs, Posts and Telecommunications.

medium-sized local authorities to host international cultural events to broaden civic international perspectives, according to a survey conducted by the Council of Local Authorities for International Relations (2001).

However, the 1990s witnessed the end of the bubble economy and found local authorities in financial straits; since fiscal year 1995, they have been forced to severely trim their budgets (fig. 1) and reassess the community benefits of international activities.

On top of these budgetary cutbacks, local authorities also have to cater for the rapidly increasing number of foreign residents in their communities. So, while Japanese local authorities have long hosted overseas visitors and study visits as a way of promoting mutual understanding and goodwill with their overseas counterparts, they are now having to reformulate their international activities and adapt to the phenomenon of globalization.

## A HISTORICAL PERSPECTIVE

In December 1955, ten years after World War II had ended, Japanese communities resumed their international activities when the city of Nagasaki and the U.S. city of St. Paul concluded a sister-city affiliation. As antiwar sentiment and pacifist movements gained momentum in Japan,[3] requests from U.S. citizens for sister-city affiliations were welcomed as an opportunity to establish international friendship at the grass-roots level.[4]

During the postwar era, Japan considered it vital, in the interests of national security and economic development, to maintain close ties with the United States, which was the most advanced industrialized nation. In the 1950s and 1960s, postwar Japanese popular culture was greatly influenced by the United States, both through American TV dramas and the heavy coverage given the country by the mass media. Therefore, with having a sister city in the United States being considered nothing short of an honor by the Japanese,[5] numerous cities felt encouraged to follow the example of Nagasaki. In fact, over 70 percent of all sister affiliations in the 1960s had their counterparts in the United States (table 2).

**Table 2.** Sister Affiliations with the United States (as of the end of each fiscal year)

|  | 1955 | 1960 | 1965 | 1970 | 1975 | 1980 | 1985 | 1990 | 1995 | 2000 | 2001 |
|---|---|---|---|---|---|---|---|---|---|---|---|
| United States | 1 | 30 | 66 | 95 | 118 | 147 | 193 | 277 | 372 | 419 | 424 |
| All affiliations | 1 | 39 | 98 | 164 | 252 | 373 | 570 | 844 | 1,189 | 1,374 | 1,407 |

*Source:* Council of Local Authorities for International Relations (2001).

At the time, local governments were almost the only agents providing citizens with opportunities for international exchange; besides Korean and Chinese immigrants, there were very few foreign visitors or residents in Japan.[6] Although the Japanese economy had long been greatly dependent on external relationships, the country was historically insular and so only local governments were systematically providing citizens with international links. Sister affiliations provided opportunities for direct interaction between local Japanese communities and overseas nationals, although only those from the higher echelons of Japanese society could at that time afford to participate in exchange opportunities.[7] Overseas travel was regarded as a luxury before the 1970s, so only high-ranking local government officials, local politicians, and businessmen were able to go abroad through sister-affiliation programs.

Since the 1970s, however, as incomes have risen, ordinary citizens have gradually begun to participate in sister-affiliation programs, local citizens and students being eager to visit their opposite numbers and experience other cultures. It was as part of the sister-affiliation programs[8] that hosting homestays became popular in the 1970s.

During the same period, local governments started cooperative arrangements with developing countries. In 1971, the Ministry of Foreign Affairs set up a grant program to allow prefectural governments to invite technical trainees from developing countries to spend several months in Japan for training.[9] Initially, prefectural governments invited over the individuals of Japanese descent from South American countries, to which many Japanese had emigrated from the early twentieth century until the 1970s.[10] Thereafter, the local governments invited trainees from other Asian countries and Africa. The Japan International Cooperation Agency (JICA) sought cooperation with local governments so as to learn from their broad knowhow of local administration, something much needed in developing countries. It was through the hosting of overseas trainees of their own and JICA's that prefectures and major cities gradually accumulated the experience necessary to become involved in broader international cooperation.

In the late 1970s, international exchange activities took center stage when Governor Nagasu Kazuji[11] of Kanagawa prefecture advocated people-to-people diplomacy, a policy that emphasized the role of local governments as international actors independent from the national government. He believed that local authorities could contribute to international relations by cultivating the solidarity of grass-roots citizens across borders and so build a peaceful world.

Gradually, other local governments also began to see international exchange as a way of invigorating their communities in terms not only of economic benefits, but also of volunteers and nonprofit organizations centering on international exchange activities. At the same time, international exchange programs were also viewed as important tools to help students learn English by enabling them to have direct contact with English speakers.

In the 1980s, overseas affiliation diversified as Japanese cities and prefectures started to form sister affiliations in East and Southeast Asian nations, which are geographically closer and culturally more familiar than Western countries. After the normalization of diplomatic relations with South Korea in 1965 and China in 1972, both these

Table 3. Sister Affiliations with China and South Korea (as of the end of each fiscal year)

|  | 1955 | 1960 | 1965 | 1970 | 1975 | 1980 | 1985 | 1990 | 1995 | 2000 | 2001 |
|---|---|---|---|---|---|---|---|---|---|---|---|
| China | 0 | 0 | 0 | 0 | 5 | 22 | 89 | 133 | 224 | 266 | 273 |
| South Korea | 0 | 0 | 0 | 2 | 7 | 12 | 22 | 39 | 63 | 75 | 96 |
| All affiliations | 1 | 39 | 98 | 164 | 252 | 373 | 570 | 844 | 1,189 | 1,374 | 1,407 |

*Source:* Council of Local Authorities for International Relations (2001).

countries emerged as major partners of Japanese local authorities (table 3).[12]

The decade of the 1980s saw many regional linkages spring up around the Sea of Japan, with prefectures vigorously competing to become the hub of interaction with affiliates on the other side of the Sea of Japan, namely, China, South Korea, the Russian Republic, and even North Korea. Historically, the Sea of Japan coast has been a gateway to the continent, and Japan has prospered as a result of exchanges with those areas in the past. But, after World War II, those relationships were discontinued as communism spread in continental Asia and memories of the war lingered. Once opportunities to create linkages with the region again appeared in the 1970s, prefectures along the Sea of Japan coast became active in promoting economic and cultural interaction by establishing sister affiliations. For the past few decades, they have organized various annual international meetings for mayors and governors in the region. Economic reasons are the main motivation behind the creation of a regional forum among local government leaders. Today Niigata, Toyama, and Tottori prefectures are the most active. Even in North Korea, with which Japan has no diplomatic relations, the city of Sakaiminato in Tottori established a sisterhood relationship with Wonsan in 1992, based on their fishery connections.

To better enable local initiatives to promote international exchange, the Ministry of Home Affairs and other ministries in 1988 created the Council of Local Authorities for International Relations (CLAIR) as the national coordination center for local governments' international initiatives.[13] The center acts as a consultant for local government bodies on international cooperation, and helps match Japanese cities with suitable overseas partners. CLAIR also initiated the Japan Education and Teaching (JET) Programme, which annually invites thousands of young people to Japan to teach foreign languages, especially English, at local junior and senior high schools.[14]

In the early 1990s, local governments established a number of international exchange associations to host international cultural events for the benefit of local citizens. While international associations worked directly with the citizens, the task of local governments remained the formulation of policies and protocol for officials, as well as making contact with overseas partners such as sister organizations.

The number of new sister affiliations increased steadily until the early 1990s, reaching 80 in fiscal year 1992 before stagnating in the latter half of the decade, the number of sister cities created yearly having declined in fiscal 2000 to less than half the figure registered in the early 1990s, the result mainly of government budget cuts. International programs were vulnerable because they did not create clear, easily measurable benefits, and did not have strong citizen support compared to such issues as education or public works. Local governments were, thus, forced to reexamine the goals and benefits of their programs.

## INTERNATIONAL ACTIVITIES AND PROGRAMS

According to the statistics by the Ministry of Public Management, Home Affairs, Posts and Telecommunications, local governments alone spent ¥104.4 billion on overseas-related activities in fiscal year 2000. Of this figure, ¥42 billion was devoted to advancing international understanding on the part of local residents by means of the JET Programme, cultural events and seminars for local residents, and grants given to grass-roots nongovernmental organizations (NGOs).

Some ¥33.7 billion was allocated for international exchange programs including overseas trips arranged by local authorities for their citizens, and arrangements for visitors from abroad. In addition, ¥10.5 billion was devoted to such activities as foreign residents' programs, scholarships for foreign students, and the promotion of international tourism. Finally, ¥7.4 billion was spent on international cooperation-related activities, such as hosting overseas trainees and sending professionals to developing countries. The remaining ¥10.8 billion was set aside for the maintenance of offices overseas and overseas study tours for Japanese local government officials.

Local governments have for many years stressed the need to increase international understanding among Japanese since the country remains insular and its people lack an international perspective. There is thus a perceived need to cultivate an international mindset and English-language speaking skills in order to survive in this increasingly interdependent world. Illustrative of the activities being undertaken by local authorities, the international programs of Miyazaki prefecture and Jōetsu city are discussed below.

### *Miyazaki Prefecture*

The economy of Miyazaki prefecture,[15] on the island of Kyushu, is based on agriculture. With a population of 1.18 million, its total budget for fiscal year 1999 was ¥668.9 billion, of which ¥3.14 billion (0.47 percent) went for international programs. The three main pillars of these programs are (1) building a society that is open to the world, (2) promotion of international exchanges and cooperation, and (3) promoting the prefecture's industries (Miyazaki Prefecture 2000).

In terms of budget, the first pillar was by far the largest in fiscal year 1999, and accounted for ¥2,533 million (80.7 percent of the international programs' budget). Some ¥1,633 million of this was used to upgrade the prefecture's seaport facilities and campaign to have Miyazaki airport made an international facility. Then ¥513 million was used for human resource building, whereby people would be enabled to develop international perspectives, and for which there are 35 programs conducted by 19 bodies (Miyazaki Prefecture 2000).

Out of these 35 programs, 22 were overseas study missions, for people ranging from female leaders of the farming community to police officers. A third portion of the budget, comprising ¥387 million, was used to create an environment in which non-Japanese and local Japanese residents can live together comfortably. The programs included the management of the Miyazaki International Center which, among its various services, provides cultural events and information for local citizens who are interested in international exchange.

The second pillar of the international programs, promoting international exchanges and cooperation, in turn has three components. The main one is the promotion of educational and cultural exchanges, and had a fiscal year 1999 budget of ¥240 million. This category included a seminar on Kyushu and Asian culture for both Japanese youth and overseas students, and the Miyazaki Music Festival.

The second component was overseas exchanges with areas with which Miyazaki has strong ties, although the prefecture did not yet have any sister affiliations. The funds for this category were also used for such contributions as that made to the Miyazaki Brazil Association and the Miyazaki-South Korea Goodwill Tree Planting Mission. International cooperation was the last component, with a budget of ¥43 million, which included hosting technical trainees from developing countries and local government interns from other Asian countries.

The third and last pillar was the promotion of industry, as part of which eleven international tourism- and convention-related programs were budgeted at ¥166 million and included incentive funds to attract international conventions. One component program was industrial internationalization which, with a budget of ¥94 million, supported Miyazaki's office in Hong Kong and allowed Miyazaki Week to be hosted in Taiwan.

## Jōetsu City

This city in Niigata prefecture, facing the Sea of Japan, has a population of 134,000 and three sister cities: Pohang in South Korea, Hunchun in China, and Lilienfeld in Austria. The city's total fiscal year 2000 budget was ¥54.37 billion, of which ¥58.6 million (0.1 percent) was set aside for use by the city's International Affairs Department. The city's biggest program that year involved sending ten junior and senior high school students to Australia for about ten days, and ten junior and senior high school students each to Italy and the United Kingdom for eleven days.

The second-largest chunk of its budget was spent on the Jōetsu International Network (JOIN), which provides a variety of programs including language-training—foreign languages for Japanese citizens and Japanese for residents from overseas—classes at which the cooking of food from various countries is taught, seminars on international awareness, Japanese speech contests for residents from overseas, and counseling services for non-Japanese residents.

The third largest program involved the hosting of trainees from Jōetsu's sister cities, Pohang and Hunchun. A local government official from each of these cities spent a year working for Jōetsu City Hall as a trainee in the International Affairs Division. The next biggest financial outlay went on hosting the orchestra visiting from Pohang.

The remainder of the funds were spent on hiring international coordinators in the JET Programme and sending a delegation to the mayors' conference of the Sea of Japan rim region.

The above description of two local governments' international activities illustrates the basic pattern followed by most local authorities. It is noticeable that they have been able to conduct overseas missions involving both local government officers and members of the general public. Such missions are often regarded as unnecessary in urban areas, where residents travel overseas extensively without much assistance, but the facilitation by local governments of student travel overseas, especially to visit sister communities, is still very common throughout Japan.

JOIN plays an important role in reaching out to citizens. Jōetsu city built a new facility, Citizens Plaza, into which JOIN moved in March

2001. It is open to all residents, both Japanese and foreign, and provides a variety of services, including the supply of information and the running of language and culture classes.

Along with promoting international understanding at the grassroots level, local government authorities are gradually coping with such new challenges of globalization as an increase in foreign residents and economic revitalization through the promotion of international tourism and trade. Here the JOIN plays an important part by, for example, working closely with such citizens' groups as Friendship Jōetsu that provides Japanese-language classes for foreign residents.

## THE IMPACT OF GLOBALIZATION

The word internationalization refers to the phenomenon of easier flow of goods across national borders. It is often used to express the efforts by which the Japanese can become more accountable and culturally understandable to the rest of the world. The international activities undertaken by local authorities have often been taken as measures leading to internationalization. In that sense, artificial efforts have often been made to make local communities more open and accessible to foreigners.

However, the term globalization, as it affects the world, refers to the phenomena created by the free flow of goods, finance, people, and information across national borders. Whereas internationalization is basically a virtue and is controlled by people, globalization seems less controllable and has both positive and negative effects. Globalization began to have an impact on Japan in the 1990s, when local governments found themselves facing new challenges that were having profound effects on communities. Several of these new challenges are discussed below.

### Multiculturalism

In the 1990s, Japan faced a new wave of globalization marked by an increase in the number of foreign residents that had begun in the late 1980s and has had major ramifications for local communities.[16] Given the unclear national policies toward immigrants, local governments have had to find their own ways of tackling the surge of newcomers. The international exchange associations together with civic groups have provided new arrivals with a raft of services—including Japanese-language training and advice on issues ranging from garbage collection to legal matters—and have worked closely with newly created citizens' groups that volunteer to help foreigners.

The issues that concern foreign residents of Japan vary widely according to the individuals' respective backgrounds. Thus, for example, there are many Koreans and Chinese who were brought to Japan during and before World War II but who do not have Japanese nationality. Those people and their descendants have been granted special status visas, are permanent residents of Japan, and must pay taxes—but they are not allowed to vote in either national or local elections. The question of whether this section of the populace should be enfranchised, at least at the local level, is currently being debated.

Then, among the new arrivals, there are many South Americans of Japanese descent who have been legally able to do any type of work, including manual labor, since the immigration law was amended in 1990. In 2000, there were 254,000 Brazilians of Japanese descent living in Japan and working predominantly in factories. The main challenges these people face are educating their children, paying for medical insurance, and getting used to the working conditions in the depressed economy (Japan Immigration Association 2001).

The city of Hamamatsu, with a population of 590,000, has the largest Brazilian community in Japan, numbering 12,000. The hometown of Yamaha Corporation, Hamamatsu is a typical industrial city located in Shizuoka prefecture. In May 2001, Hamamatsu urged twelve other cities that also have many residents from South America to join the newly created Committee for Localities with a Concentrated Foreigner Population, a grouping of cities in Japan in which South Americans of Japanese descent live. It hopes to exchange views with these cities on how to deal with foreign residents, and formulate proposals for the central government.[17]

Another type of foreign resident is the individual who remains in Japan beyond the time allowed by their visa. Such people often come to Japan on a tourist visa and then find work at, for example, construction

sites, in night clubs, or in factories. Their living standards are often
low and they face a variety of problems, including being the target of
crime and having their human rights violated. As many as 232,000
overstayers, as they are known, were believed to be living in Japan as of
January 2001.[18]

## Economic Globalization

Japanese local governments did not initially seek economic benefits
as their primary goal when forming sister affiliations for, while local
manufacturers were highly dependent on exports, the major trading
companies in the big cities had mostly been responsible for external
transactions. Therefore, local businesses had generally had only limited exposure to and experiences in the conduct of international business until recently.

The impact of economic globalization began to be felt keenly at
the grass-roots level in the 1990s, with the emasculation of domestic
manufacturing industries. To circumvent the high domestic wages,
Japanese industries began shifting their plants offshore to China and
Southeast Asia, where the industrial infrastructure had improved but
wages were lower than in Japan.

In the 1980s, big Japanese corporations and their subsidiaries
had invested heavily in the United States, and then in the 1990s, local
Japanese industries began to invest in other Asian countries in a bid to
survive. Economic competition drove some 40 percent of Japanese
export manufacturing capacity offshore. Figures for 1997 show that
in Toyama prefecture, located on the Sea of Japan coast and with a
population of 1.12 million, 149 companies had 178 overseas offices in
48 countries and regions (Toyama Kokusai Sentā 1998). There were
19 Toyama companies with 22 offices in China, 18 companies with 27
offices in the United States, and ten companies with 13 offices in Hong
Kong, followed by a lesser number of companies in Singapore, Ma-
laysia, South Korea, and Taiwan.

Japanese local governments also set up foreign offices and so, according to a 1997 survey by the then Home Ministry, 31 prefectures
and seven cities had set up 103 overseas offices, while ten other municipalities had also set up offices overseas. And, compared with a similar
survey conducted in 1987, the number of overseas representative

offices that handled business-related matters and international exchange arrangements had tripled during the decade to 1997.

Japan's agriculture sector has been severely hit by imports of inexpensive food items from China and East Asian countries, as a result of which safeguard measures were, in 2000, imposed on imports of *shiitake* mushrooms, leek, and *igusa* (the rush used in tatami mats) from China. Clearly, there are no measures in place to protect Japanese agricultural communities from such inexpensive imports.[19]

Japan has reacted to the pressures of the global economy by attracting foreign investments, but this, too, has had a negative side: Most of the investments have been made in Tokyo, which, in 2000, accounted for 77.0 percent of the foreign investment in the country, some 3,320 foreign companies having set up their headquarters in Tokyo. This is in sharp contrast with, for example, Tottori prefecture, which until 2000 had not one foreign company or factory, and Shimane prefecture, which had only one factory (Tōyō Keizai Shimpō-sha 1998). Nevertheless, foreign investment in Japan has increased over the past five years, having risen from ¥433 billion in fiscal year 1994 to ¥2,399 billion in fiscal year 1999, due to the deregulation of domestic laws and regulations, and the subsequent expansion of foreign financial and telecommunications companies (Masuda and Tanabe 2001).

In a bid to have its share of the investment pie, Hyōgo prefecture established the Hyōgo Investment Support Center in 1999 to allow foreign companies to rent office space at low rates, and has provided consultation services for these customers. Yokohama city, in turn, succeeded in attracting U.K. companies when it set up the British Industry Centre in 1997 in the Yokohama Business Park. And even the remote Shimane prefecture, situated on the Sea of Japan coast, has felt prompted to invite foreign investors, to which end it has published a report suggesting that the prefectural government should focus on Chinese and South Korean corporations (Shimane-ken Gaishi-kei Kigyō 2001).

Since the 1990s, the domestic labor force has undergone major changes and foreign workers have become indispensable in the prefectures of Gunma and Shizuoka, where manufacturing is the main industry. Without these workers—mainly comprising South American workers, Asians with training visas, and overstayers—the many small and medium-sized manufacturers would be unable to remain in business.

## International Cooperation with Asia

In the early 1970s, several prefectures began to assist developing countries by inviting technical trainees from overseas. The technical trainee programs have been financially supported by the Ministry of Foreign Affairs. Prefectures usually invited trainees from South America where many Japanese emmigrated for decades.

Since the 1980s, local governments have stepped up their overseas cooperation, and have paid greater attention to developing countries, especially in Asia. At about the same time, the mass media began to cover issues in Asian and other developing countries, rather than the United States and Europe, as they had earlier been wont to do. Just before this, international NGOs, organized by citizens to give assistance in developing countries, began to mushroom in Japan, interest in the region having been piqued by the arrival of Indochinese refugees in the late 1970s.[20]

During the 1980s and 1990s, Chinese cities that had sister affiliations with Japanese local governments sought assistance from, and collaboration with, their Japanese counterparts. Not stopping at the technical trainee programs, authorities in both countries expanded the scope of their exchanges, Japanese technical experts visiting sister cities and Chinese visiting Japan on study trips.

Okayama prefecture, a sister affiliate of Jiangxi province in China, invited two forestry technicians from Jiangxi to visit for three weeks and sent two of its own forestry experts to tackle forestry problems in its sister province. Okayama prefecture also invited junior high school students from Jiangxi to come over and discuss environmental protection issues with Okayama students. Further, Okayama prefecture has worked with a local NGO, the Association of Medical Doctors of Asia (AMDA), and invited high school students to come and discuss international cooperation and volunteering. In this connection, the prefecture and the Okayama International Center in 2000 co-hosted the International Contribution Forum, to which it invited local NGO representatives as panelists to discuss the theme "Okayama—Open to the World, Cooperating with All People." As can be seen from the above examples, international cooperation has increasingly come to involve local citizens and NGOs.

Miyazaki prefecture started a technical trainee program in 1980, later than most other prefectures. Nearly half its trainees even now come from Brazil, with which Miyazaki has an immigration relationship, and are trained at such prefectural facilities as the hospital, agricultural research center, agricultural training institute, husbandry experimentation center, and the construction technology center. In addition, private companies, including a shipping company, a timber company, and a computer software company, host trainees, something that major local corporations like Miyazaki Bank, Miyazaki Broadcasting Corp., and Miyazaki Kohtsū Co. used to do in the past. More recently, Miyazaki prefecture started a program to send technical staff to Asian countries, and in 1998, four members of the prefecture's staff were sent to Nepal to teach farmers about sweet fish farming.

Local governments are motivated to conduct international cooperation activities for a variety of reasons. Niigata prefecture, for example, in 1997 formulated the Niigata International Cooperation Promotion Guidelines that outline its goals:

- To make Niigata the focus of the Sea of Japan rim region and to use international cooperation to strengthen its relationship with other nearby Asian countries.
- To ensure that regions along the Sea of Japan rim share their know-how and technology to combat common and mutually detrimental challenges, such as acid rain and ocean pollution.
- To help local governments apply their local know-how and give advice to needy areas.
- To identify local characteristics and revitalize local industries.
- To help citizens in the prefecture develop an international mindset and nurture global perspectives.

These guidelines also set forth six main pillars on which Niigata's goals were to be based, namely, that (1) the Sea of Japan rim is the key area of focus; (2) a spirit of sharing and harmonious existence must be engendered; (3) humanitarian considerations must be paramount; (4) a spirit of equal partnership must be encouraged; (5) a multifaceted approach must be taken so that Niigata's resources might be fully utilized; and (6) all citizens must be encouraged to participate. Niigata's case illustrates the difference between official development assistance (ODA) extended by the national government and international cooperation extended by a local government. Whereas national government assistance is basically one-sided, local governments try to create mutual benefits based on an equal footing with their counterparts in developing countries. Also, citizens are encouraged to participate to deepen intercultural understanding and aid activities, by using local resources and characteristics.

## CHALLENGES AND OPPORTUNITIES

The challenges of globalization have enticed Japanese local government authorities onto a new stage, as they contemplate the effects and impact of globalization and assess how best to capitalize on the opportunities as they unfold.

If they are to achieve a society tolerant of cultural diversity, it is imperative that local communities and governments take the new challenges seriously. Japan's homogenous society has so far reacted with equanimity, but the degree of diversity is expected to increase and, should economic conditions deteriorate further, there may well be friction between Japanese and foreign citizens.

So, at this juncture, the efforts of Hamamatsu are indeed relevant; local authorities, which are expected to make the living environment amenable to both Japanese and foreign residents, are now realizing that they get the best results in terms of reaching out and cost effectiveness when they work closely with civic groups and nonprofit organizations (NPOs) in the community.

Adjusting to the maelstrom of economic globalization requires that well-orchestrated and carefully thought-out efforts by local governments be made in conjunction with the private sector, so that new business opportunities can be found at the grass-roots level. Other Asian countries will inevitably be involved and increasingly become important partners as local governments explore ways of creating mutually beneficial relationships.

Through greater international cooperation Japanese communities will strengthen their ties overseas, particularly in Asia and, as they become more aware of the potential of their Asian neighborhood, benefits of grass-roots exchanges should accrue for both sides. Moreover, in order to cope with such global issues as environmental problems and the aging population, local authorities in Japan also need to strengthen their relationship with the United States and other advanced countries.

Although sister affiliations with the United States date back the furthest and number the largest, they are now no longer always particularly beneficial. Both Japanese and U.S. cities need to discuss how the relationships might be revitalized so that the new challenges may be better handled at the practical level through, for example, e-commerce and e-education.

But surmounting the new hurdles requires that Japanese local authorities be ready for the changes. The majority, however, are not. Many local authorities lack a clear sense of direction regarding where their international activities are heading. International activities have been conventionally regarded as festive events or "something good to do." Clarification of their goals is important given their financial problems and the effect that globalization is having on communities.

Local governments usually have only a very small number of specialists in international affairs and staff members are usually rotated to different divisions every three years or so. The lack of qualified staff is accountable for the poor achievement of grass-roots exchanges. With better-trained staff, local governments can get a better grasp of international policy and establish more comprehensive programs. Local authorities will increasingly find themselves being requested to work with other sectors, especially NPOs and the business community, and, as the impact of globalization comes to affect citizens in an ever-growing variety of ways, communities will become the hubs that coordinate international activities. Economic globalization is changing the organizational balance of power in communities and the leadership structures. Borders and traditions are becoming less relevant and increasing competition is challenging traditional leadership assumptions. As the world moves toward a global economy, communities are being presented with multiple options that are fueling the push to self-decision at the local level, and thus decentralization will continue to influence structural relationships throughout Japanese society.

The question remains whether it will be local government authorities or other civic actors who will take the lead and set the agenda in communities rapidly being transformed by a shift in societal values, the impact of globalization, and the very structure of how businesses operate. A collective, networked force and a jointly created and shared vision at the local level are needed if there is to be a systematic and strategic approach to globalization.

## NOTES

1. The Ministry of Home Affairs, after incorporating other ministries, was renamed the Ministry of Public Management, Home Affairs, Posts and Tele-communications in January 2001.

2. Called *chiiki kokusaika kyōkai* in Japanese, they were set up by local government authorities and given such names as the Iwate International Asso-ciation, the Oita International Center, and the Osaka Foundation for Interna-tional Exchange. According to a survey conducted by the Council of Local Authorities for International Relations (CLAIR) in 2000, a total of 59 prefec-tures and several designated cities had established local international exchange associations that had a staff of 1,482 and an average annual budget of ¥500 million.

3. The peace movement became politicized during the cold war era and, together with the antinuclear movement, was supported by the Japan Socialist Party in opposition to the U.S.-Japan Security Treaty. With the end of the cold war, both movements lost steam.

4. The origin of sister-city affiliations can be traced back to relationships between communities in Europe and those in the United States to which citi-zens of the former had migrated. The affiliations began as natural linkages between people in communities that transcended national borders. However, since the mid-1950s, the U.S. government has promoted sister-city affiliations as a feature of its overseas diplomacy. At a White House conference in 1956, President Dwight D. Eisenhower proposed a people-to-people program at a time when U.S.-Soviet tensions had eased somewhat, and the sister-city affilia-tions became the mainstay of the program. In the 1950s, U.S. government agencies located in Japan took the initiative of creating sister affiliations among Nagoya–Los Angeles, Kobe-Seattle, and Okayama–San Jose.

5. American visitors to Japanese sister cities were often overwhelmed by the enthusiastic welcome they received and were often paraded down the main street while crowds waved American and Japanese flags.

6. In 1965, there were 291,000 visitors to Japan from abroad. The number increased to 775,000 in 1970, 780,000 in 1975, and 1.3 million in 1980 (Immi-gration Bureau 1998). After World War II, many of the Koreans and Chinese who had been forcibly brought to Japan before and during the war decided to remain in Japan. In 2000, there were some 635,000 Koreans and 336,000 Chi-nese residing in Japan (Japan Immigration Association 2001).

7. Following World War II, ordinary citizens were not allowed to travel abroad until 1964, when 120,000 Japanese did so. Since then, the number of Japanese traveling overseas has increased rapidly, having reached 17.82 million in 2000.

8. In 1968, Sapporo City in Hokkaido inaugurated the first homestay pro-gram organized by a local government by hosting visitors from its sister city, Portland, Oregon.

9. In 1971, the prefectures of Yamanashi, Hyōgo, and Kumamoto availed themselves of a government grant, while in fiscal year 1999, all 47 prefectures and five designated cities participated in the grant program, inviting 594 technical trainees from developing countries to visit. In the same year and in addition to the grant program, local governments hosted 790 technical trainees who were sponsored by the Japan International Cooperation Agency (JICA). JICA also sponsored a technical specialists' dispatch program, according to which Japanese were to be recruited from local government and sent to developing countries. In fiscal year 1999, more than 200 specialists were recruited.

10. Some 240,000 Japanese emigrated to Brazil during that period.

11. Nagasu was a socialist professor-turned-governor who was first elected in 1975 and remained Kanagawa governor for twenty years. He proclaimed the Age of Regions, emphasizing the autonomy of local government.

12. The first sister-city link with South Korea was set up in 1968 between Hagi-shi, in Yamaguchi prefecture, and Ulsan. Kobe was the first to set up a sister-city affiliation with China, setting up ties with Tianjin in 1973.

13. The other ministries involved were the Ministry of Education, Science, Sports and Culture and the Ministry of Foreign Affairs. The leadership of CLAIR has been kept in the hands of the Ministry of Home Affairs (currently, the Ministry of Public Management, Home Affairs, Posts and Telecommunications).

14. In fiscal year 2000, CLAIR invited 6,078 people from 39 countries. There are three job categories in the JET Progamme, namely, Assistant Language Teacher (ALT), Coordinator for International Relations (CIR), and Sports Exchange Advisor (SEA). ALTs are under the supervision of the education boards of local governments and teach at local schools. Five languages are taught by ALTs: English, French, German, Chinese, and Korean. The CIRs and SEAs are usually under the supervision of local government authorities. See <http://www.jetprogramme.org/index.html>.

15. See Miyazaki Prefecture (2000). Also see <http://www.pref.miyazaki jp/english/index.htm> for more information on Miyazaki prefecture. In the 1960s, the prefecture was a popular destination for couples on their honeymoon. Tourism has remained Miyazaki's major industry due to its warm and sunny climate, and over the past few years it has also attracted tourists from overseas.

16. In 1985, there were 841,000 registered foreigners residing in Japan; in 2000, the figure had risen to around 1.7 million.

17. Issues such as labor, education, medical treatment, and social welfare have been discussed among the member cities. The member cities are Hamamatsu, Iwata, Kosai, and Fuji (joined later) in Shizuoka prefecture; Toyohashi and Toyoda in Aichi prefecture; Yokkaichi and Suzuka in Mie prefecture; Ōgaki, Kani, and Minokamo in Gifu prefecture; Ōta and Ōizumi in Gunma prefecture; and Iida in Nagano prefecture.

18. Besides overstayers, who initially came to Japan with a passport and visa, there are also a number of illegal immigrants living in the country who originally arrived by boat and circumvented the immigration authorities (Suzuki 2001).

19. Some Japanese corporations are even believed to have cooperated with Chinese companies in setting up vegetable farms for the purpose of exporting the produce to Japan.

20. For information on the international activities of Japanese NGOs, see <http://www.geocities.co.jp/WallStreet/3294/ngodata.html>.

## BIBLIOGRAPHY

Council of Local Authorities for International Relations. 2000. "Shimai teikei no dōkō ni tsuite" (Trends of sister city affiliations). *Jichitai Kokusaika Fōramu* 129 (July): 20–21.

———. 2001. *Japanese Local Government International Affiliation Directory*. Tokyo: Council of Local Authorities for International Relations.

Gerrit, Jan Schep, Frank Angenent, Jeroen Wismans, and Michel Hillenius. 1995. *Local Challenges to Global Change*. The Hague: Sdu Publishers.

Immigration Bureau. 1998. *Shutsunyūkoku kanri* (Immigration control). Tokyo: Ministry of Justice.

Japan Immigration Association. 2001. *Zairyū gaikokujin tōkei* (Statistics on registered foreigners). Tokyo: Japan Immigration Association.

Masuda Kōtarō and Tanabe Atsuko. 2001. "Kyūzō suru tainichi tōshigaku no kokusai hikaku" (International comparison of growing investment to Japan). *ITI Kihō*, no. 44. <http://www.iti.or.jp/kiho44/44masudatanabe.pdf> (10 December 2002).

Menju Toshihiro. 1997. *Chikyū shimin nettowāku* (Networking for global citizenship). Tokyo: ALC Press.

———. 1998a. "Jichitai gaikō no susume" (International diplomacy of local governments). Tokyo: *Chūōkōron* (October): 204–214.

——— 1998b. "Jichitai no kokusai kōken" (International contribution of local authorities). In *Chihōjichi no sentanriron* (Advanced theories for local governments). Tokyo: Keisō Shobō.

———. 1998c. "Shimaitoshi kōryū towa" (The exchange of sister city affiliation). In Sapporo Education Board, ed. *Shimaitoshi* (Sister cities). Sapporo: Sapporo Bunko.

———. 1999a. "A New Paradigm of North-South Relationship: Implications of International Cooperation by Local Authorities in Japan." In Inoguchi Takashi, Edward Newman, and Glen Paolett, eds. *Cities and the Environment: New Approaches for Eco-Societies*. Tokyo: United Nations University Press.

———. 1999b. "Kokusaikyōryoku kokusaikōryū to NPO" (International cooperation and international exchange by NPOs). In Nakamura Yōichi and Nihon NPO Center eds. *Nihon no NPO 2000* (Japan's NPOs 2000). Tokyo: Nihon Hyōronsha.

————. 1999c. "Gurōbarizeishon to chiikishakai, NPO" (Globalization, local communities and NPOs). *Jichi Fōramu* (July): 16–21.

————. 1999d. "Shiminkōryū ga kokusaikankei wo kaeru" (Impact on international relations by citizens' international exchange). *Gaikō Fōramu* (March 1999): 52–57.

Miyazaki Prefecture. 2000. "Miyazaki-ken no kokusaika no genjō" (Present state of Miyazaki's internationalization). Report issued by the prefecture's International Affairs Division.

Shimane-ken Gaishi-kei Kigyō Yūchi Senryaku Kenkyū-kai. 2001. "Shimane-ken Gaishi-kei Kigyō Yūchi Senryaku Kenkyū-kai hōkokusho" (Report of Shimane-ken Gaishi-kei Kigyō Yūchi Senryaku Kenkyū-kai). <http://www.pref.shimane.jp/section/kishin/gaishi/houkoku.html> (in Japanese only).

Suzuki Eriko. 2001. "Nihon ni okeru tabunkashugi no jitsugen ni mukete" (Toward realization of multiculturalism in Japan). *FIF Monograph*, no. 4-1. Published by the Fujita Institute of Future Management Research.

Toyama Kokusai Sentā, ed. 1998. *Toyama-ken kigyō no kaigai jigyōsho chōsa* (Survey of overseas business operations in Toyama prefecture). Toyama, Japan: Toyama Kokusai Sentā.

Tōyō Keizai Shimpō-sha. 1998. *Gaishi-kei kigyō sōran 1998* (Directory of foreign-affiliated firms). Tokyo: Tōyō Keizai Shimpō-sha.

Yoshida Hitoshi. 2000. *Chihōjichitai no kokusaikyōryoku* (International cooperation by local authorities). Tokyo: Nihon Hyōronsha.

# 5

# Think Tanks in a Changing Regional Environment

## Nakamura Madoka

Japan has frequently been criticized for its highly centralized government, in which powerful bureaucrats in the national ministries dominate the policy process, planning and controlling most local policy issues. However, as society is becoming decentralized, think tanks have come to assume greater significance as public policy institutes, bridging and linking policy research with existing issues.

In April 2000, the Omnibus Law of Decentralization took effect, clearly defining the autonomy of local governments from the central government. In principle, local governments are now in charge of local and regional public policies independent of the central ministries, and so are responsible for all aspects of policy planning, including policy formulation, decision making, as well as policy implementation and evaluation. The Omnibus Law of Decentralization also laid the groundwork for developing guidelines to promote the formulation of local policies by other policy actors, namely, the public, nonprofit organizations (NPOs), and policy think tanks.

The participation of and cooperation with such independent policy actors is essential in a decentralized society, just as policy pluralism is fundamental to and indispensable in self-governance. Thus, despite the centralized bureaucracy, the regional and local think tank community has been expanding in Japan. Each prefecture has its policy institutes, which seek to contribute to the regional and local policy process. Regional and plural policy infrastructures not only enable local government authorities to better plan policy, but they also serve to attract the participation of independent policy actors, thereby making it possible for alternate ideas to be adopted from a variety of policy debates. Such cooperation is important in the regional and local policy process, given that the issues discussed usually directly affect the communities involved, and requires a regional—rather than centralized—framework.

## THINK TANKS TODAY

The existence of think tanks in Japan dates back to the first half of the 1970s, and there are currently some 400 such institutions.

In the latest survey, there was a roughly even number of for-profit corporate and nonprofit foundation or association think tanks. However, since 81 percent of the staff and 70 percent of the researchers belong to the for-profit sector, Japanese think tanks are generally considered to be for-profit corporate entities. Some 80 percent of all think-tank research is commissioned (table 1), mainly by the national government or regional and administrative authorities, or public organizations. The revenue derived from these is an important source of income but, with commissions decreasing recently due to the government's budgetary shortage, and the resultant competitive bidding in the selection of research institutes, think tanks are increasingly having to rely for their revenue on government subsidies, fund-related revenue, membership fees, and publication sales.

With interest rates around zero, think tanks that operate as foundations are finding it difficult to raise their own funds from endowments. Besides, while grants from domestic and overseas foundations play an insignificant part in funding policy research in Japan (National Institute for Research Advancement [NIRA] 2000), and the size of grants from Japanese foundations is miniscule and decreasing, policy

Table 1. Japanese Think Tanks: Staffing and Funding

|  | | Number of Institutes | | Staff | Researchers |
|---|---|---|---|---|---|
| A | Nonprofit | 150 | 51% | 19% | 30% |
| B | For-profit | 146 | 49% | 81% | 70% |
|  | | Funding Source | | | |
| A + B | | Commissioned | 78.2% | | |
|  | | Self-funded | 18.7% | | |
|  | | Grant funded | 3.1% | | |

*Source:* National Institute for Research Advancement (2000).

research is not popular among grant-making foundations. According to a 1999 annual survey that analyzed more than 4,000 think tank research projects, only 130 projects (3.1 percent) were funded by grants (table 1).

## THE DEVELOPMENT OF THINK TANKS

The discussions conducted by the Liberal Democratic Party (LDP) and the Ministry of International Trade and Industry (MITI) in the early 1970s shed light on the principles underlying think tanks in the past and their development since. These LDP and MITI reports, which led to the first think tank boom, assessed the institutions from a government-policy perspective as management consultants. U.S. think tanks, for example, were in 1971 classified into two main categories—wide-ranging and specialized—and subcategories; specialized think tanks were divided into laboratory- and office-based think tanks, and the latter were again divided into three subcategories: social and economic; management consulting; and system and technology (table 2). Another Japanese report of the early 1970s classified think tanks into five categories: traditional government, traditional science and technology, management consultancies, information research, and corporate research (Katagata 1970, 51–88).

According to more recent studies on think tanks worldwide, the institutions listed in the above-mentioned MITI report are generally no longer classified as think tanks, with the exception of the RAND Corporation and the Brookings Institution in the United States. Moreover, the Japanese think tank industry has developed quite differently

Table 2. MITI Classification of U.S. Think Tanks

| Classifications | | | Typical Examples |
|---|---|---|---|
| Wide-Ranging | | | RAND Corporation, Stanford Research Institute, Battelle Memorial Institute, Arthur D. Little, Inc. |
| Specialized | Laboratories | | Franklin Institute, Mellon Institute |
| | Offices | Social economic analysis | Brookings Institution, Center for the Study of Democratic Institutions |
| | | Management consulting | Booze Allen and Hamilton Co., McKinsey and Co. |
| | | System and technology | Systems Development Co., Computer Sciences Co. |

Source: Ministry of International Trade and Industry (1971).

from that of other countries, as the MITI and LDP reports were inaccurate in their predictions of future developments.

## THINK TANKS OVERSEAS

The term think tank was first used in the United States during the 1960s to describe the RAND Corporation,[1] and it is now widely accepted as synonymous with public policy research institute. However, RAND has become atypical of contemporary policy institutes, because of its close ties with the Pentagon, its research focus on science and technology, the relatively high proportion of contract research projects it handles, and its enormous size and budget. Meanwhile, the Brookings Institution remains a model think tank, with its wide-ranging policy research. According to current U.S. usage, the term think tank describes a mostly private, nonprofit, and independent institution (Stone 1996, 9–37).

In Germany, the institution of the think tank, such as the "big six economic research institutes," is well developed.[2] In contrast to U.S. think tanks, the German institutes generally receive a considerable budgetary allocation from the federal government and local governments, with only a few enjoying the financial independence of their U.S. counterparts. While policy-related research institutes are generally associated with a foundation or an interest group, think tanks in

Germany pursue a public purpose, despite their dependence on financing and management from the federal government and local authorities (Gellner 1998, 82–106). Nevertheless, they enjoy the same research autonomy and freedom as do publicly supported universities. Moreover, German think tanks provide politicians and governments with new policy ideas, and the general public with research.

In Asia, meanwhile, think tanks usually have close ties to the government and are able to influence the policymaking process. The Korea Institute for International Economic Policy (KIEP), founded in 1990, with its staff of about 100, specializes in the international economy and enjoys a role as a direct policy adviser to the South Korean government.

Think tanks worldwide have any one or some of several characteristics: they are permanent bodies, independent from governments or universities, multidisciplinary, policy-oriented, geared to a public purpose, and offer a professional level of expertise. They are generally classified into four categories: academic institutions, referred to as universities without students; contract researchers; advocacy think tanks; and party think tanks (Stone 1996, 9–24; McGann and Weaver 2000, 6–12). In addition, there are public policy research institutes that provide new ideas for politicians seeking innovative policies for elections, evaluate policies with a long-term perspective, and support administrative staff with their policy expertise. Since an important audience for think tanks is the public, most of their research is widely available.

There is as yet no hard and fast definition of a think tank, although the U.S. model is generally used as the prototype. However, due to regional differences in the social and political environment, policymaking process, political appointee system, and relationships among policy actors, the organizational status and policy research activities of think tanks differ considerably not only among but also within countries. So, while Asian institutions might not be considered independent from the government according to the U.S. definition of a think tank, they do nevertheless benefit from assured and sufficient financial support, and have a certain degree of freedom and autonomy not enjoyed by government departments and institutes. Moreover, it is their very relationship with implementing authorities that enables them to influence the public policy process.

## CHARACTERISTICS OF
## JAPANESE THINK TANKS

Created largely as a consequence of influential discussions and policy reports released in the 1970s, Japanese think tanks comprise many for-profit companies, the work of which is generally restricted to the areas of management consulting and client-commissioned projects. They have yet to be drawn into a structure to support NPOs. In other countries, think tanks are primarily public policy institutions that analyze social and economic issues based on their particular area of expertise, the Brookings Institution being a typical example; management consultants as well as scientific and technological institutions are separate categories of business.

Operating as for-profit businesses is the main characteristic that differentiates think tanks in Japan from those in other countries. Japanese think tanks are generally subsidiaries of major banks and financial institutions, or members of the former conglomerates (*zaibatsu*) that were largely disbanded following World War II, and conduct research projects exclusively for their clients, although some do conduct public policy research.

Second, 80 percent of the think tank research is conducted on a contractual basis, commissioned by businesses or governmental institutions, with projects usually individually commissioned, contracted, and strictly controlled by research agreements. This is in sharp contrast to the numerous policy institutes in the United States and Europe that do not accept contract projects.

Third, because of their dependence on government authorities and parent companies for financial and personnel resources, think tanks are unable to conduct independent research (NIRA 1997).

Fourth, most think tank research is not in the public domain, as information concerning about 85 percent of the research reports is not disclosed. In the 1999 worldwide survey of think tanks conducted by the National Institute for Research Advancement (NIRA), about 40 percent of institutes stated that they made "all" policy reports available to the public, and about 35 percent said that they made "most" of them available (NIRA 2000). The confidentiality of think tank reports is exceptionally high in Japan.

## RECONSIDERING THINK TANK ACTIVITY

Participatory policy analysis (PPA) has been proposed to improve and resolve dilemmas of traditional social analyses.[3] PPA addresses two failures of traditional analysis: its undemocratic nature and the analytical mistakes that result from its positivist framework. Traditional policy analysis was not particularly concerned with the tension between expert knowledge and democracy but, rather, was focused on experts and professional knowledge. Thus, whereas traditional policy analysts were accused of serving the interests of power elites, exploiting the masses, and helping to maintain the status quo, PPA not only encourages citizen participation, but it also involves citizens in policy-making.

There are four types of PPA, namely, that which assesses the degree of participatory democracy, facilitates the input of analyses, serves an interpretative function, or analyzes stakeholder policy. They differ in purpose and in the relationships that exist among policy actors, which include policy analysts, citizens, decision makers, and stakeholders. The PPA that assesses democratic participation gives policy analysts a direct link to citizens, while the other three types of PPA sometimes allow policy analysts to receive information from citizens, but do not necessarily provide advice or information directly to citizens (Durning 1993). The first type of PPA is the only model with direct links between policy analysts and citizens and, with the goals of empowerment, liberation, and social transformation, it shares similarities with think tanks and traditional policy analysis.

There are several reasons for policy debate being limited in Japan. First, Japanese citizens have been excessively dependent on government, and there has been little participation by outside policy actors (Miyakawa 2000). Think tanks have not been promoted to propose or provide alternative ideas in competition with or critical of government policy. With their work restricted mainly to commissioned projects that involve simply collecting data and information to confirm and verify the policies of clients such as governments, parent companies, or industry, Japanese think tanks have not supported PPA for participatory democracy.

Second, policy research as an academic discipline is not well developed in Japan. By comparison, policy studies and public policy research have long been conducted at U.S. universities, and with the advance of policy studies as a discipline, many university-affiliated think tanks have become involved in the policy process and are promoting policy discussions. Recently, Japanese universities have started to set up faculties and departments for undergraduate and postgraduate policy studies. The University of Tsukuba was the first to take the initiative in 1976, followed by Saitama University in 1977. Many other universities followed suit in the 1990s, including the Faculty of Policy Management of the Shōnan-Fujisawa Campus at Keiō University, the Faculty of Policy Studies at Chūō University, and the College of Policy Science at Ritsumeikan University. In 1997, the National Graduate Institute for Policy Studies was established to supersede the Graduate School of Policy Science at Saitama University (Miyakawa 1995; 117–121, Ōya, Ōta, and Mayama 1998, 6–9).

The third reason that policy debate is limited in Japan is that details of the policy process and related government information are rarely disclosed to the public. Only central ministries have policy-related information and it was not until April 2001 that the Law Concerning the Disclosure of Information that Administrative Organs Hold (Freedom of Information Act) was introduced, compelling the government to disclose certain types of information. Now, in the wake of the government's expanded accountability, in terms of information disclosure and policy evaluation, policy information must be studied further.

## THE DEVELOPMENT OF REGIONAL POLICY INSTITUTES

Regional think tanks exist in every Japanese prefecture and generally focus on policy issues within the region or prefecture and promote regional policy studies.[4] The Think Tank Association of Japan, established in 1985 to promote cooperation among think tanks in the area of information and research exchange, lists about 130 regional institutes throughout the country, excluding Tokyo, Chiba, Kanagawa, and Saitama prefectures. Another association, the Metropolitan Think Tank Group, comprises 12 institutions in the four prefectures. This compares with 110 state-level think tanks found in the United States (Rich 2000).

Table 3. Breakdown of Regional Think Tanks

| Type | Number | Year Set Up | Number |
|---|---|---|---|
| A  For-profit | 56 | | |
| B  Nonprofit | 73 | | |
| A + B | 129 | prior to 1959 | 2 |
| | | 1960s | 19 |
| | | 1970s | 40 |
| | | 1980s | 48 |
| | | 1990s | 20 |

*Source:* National Institute for Research Advancement (2000).

Regional and local think tanks have been set up mainly since the 1960s, with the exception of the Kyushu Economic Research Center that was founded in 1946. In the 1960s, many institutes were established under the auspices of central government ministries; in the 1970s, such institutes were established by local governments and regional banks. Then, in the 1980s, there was a regional boom in think tanks, particularly between 1986 and 1988.

Fifty-six percent of regional think tanks operate on a nonprofit basis (table 3), compared with the 51 percent of think tanks as a whole that do so, and the majority were founded by prefectural governments, in some cases in association with municipal governments or regional banks (fig. 1). Regional think tanks receive a considerable amount of

Figure 1. Regional Think Tanks by Affiliation

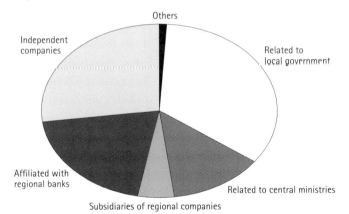

*Source:* Data from National Institute for Research Advancement (2000).

commissioned research from governmental institutions, one third of which are local authorities.

After the collapse of the bubble economy in the early 1990s, many think tanks were restructured or transformed. For example, the Yamaichi Research Institute of Securities & Economics, Inc., a subsidiary of Yamaichi Securities Co., Ltd.,[5] was closed down in January 1998, and the LTCB Research Institute, Inc., an affiliated corporation of the Long-Term Credit Bank (LTCB),[6] was transferred and renamed, following the LTCB's bankruptcy in 1998. Then, in connection with the recent restructuring of Japanese banks, a research division of the Sakura Institute of Research Inc. was merged with a department of the Japan Research Institute Ltd., following the merger of the parent companies, Sakura Bank and Sumitomo Bank. The Dentsū Institute for Human Studies, which had originally operated independently from its parent company, the advertising giant Dentsū Inc., recently became an internal division of the parent.

Outside Tokyo, the regional Takugin Research Institute was transformed into the Hokkaido Research Institute for the Twenty-First Century Co., Ltd., in the wake of the 1997 bankruptcy of the parent bank, Hokkaido Takushoku Bank.[7] The new organization operates as a regional think tank in Hokkaido, where it has financial support, and specializes in regional policy issues (NIRA 2000). By contrast, Think Tank Saitama and Mie Institute of Social Economic Research suspended operations due to the administrative reforms adopted in their respective prefectures.

Twenty new regional think tanks were established during the 1990s (table 3), including the Kochi Prefecture Policy Research Center (1992), Economic Research Institute for Northeast Asia (1993), Tottori Research Center (1995), and Yamanashi Research Institute Foundation (1998). By contrast, the industry itself did not expand significantly in the decade.

## RELATIONS WITH LOCAL GOVERNMENTS

As the number of regional think tanks has grown, so has their influence in moving the policy community toward decentralization by promoting regional policy activities, advancing policy discussions, and acting as a bridge between governments and other players in the policy process.

Despite their influence, however, think tanks still have a vertical and hierarchical relationship with local governments, the former institutions being contracted to carry out policy research projects by the latter (table 4). Local administrative staff often consider think tanks to be consultancies rather than independent public policy research institutes, for which reason administrators often seek ways of making subcontracted think tank studies useful to the local cause. Local government–related think tanks are generally government subsidiaries that rely on the government for financial and personnel resources. Further, reinforcing the hierarchical relationship between Tokyo and regional or local-area think tanks, one will sometimes even find local think tanks appointing directors from Tokyo-based institutions.

Table 4. Research Contracted to Regional Think Tanks

| Contracting Clients | % of Total Research |
|---|---|
| Central ministries | 17.6 |
| Prefectural governments | 12.2 |
| Municipal governments | 20.8 |
| Other local government-related institutions | 7.9 |
| Special-status corporations | 9.0 |
| Foundations | 17.0 |
| Business corporations | 13.0 |
| International institutions | 0.2 |
| Others | 1.9 |
| NA | 0.3 |

*Source:* National Institute for Research Advancement (2000).

Administrators will often emphasize the importance of government policy institutions as they promote the establishment of policy centers within local governments, in a bid to improve the standing of their own local authority. They recognize the need to analyze long-term policy research perspectives and the fact that, in the decentralized policy process, local governments must become powerful policy administrators. Administrators also realize that, in order to develop their own think tanks, researchers must have had a chance to experience policy administration duties, otherwise they will not be able to identify the problems and obstacles in the policy administration process or propose effective and practical policies.

## COMMISSIONED PROJECTS

With close to 80 percent of think tank research in Japan being commissioned (table 1), these institutes are clearly highly dependent financially on such projects. In the area of policy research, there are two types of contracts: one in which the contracting institution selects the policy theme, and the other in which the commissioned institute selects the theme, which allows it eventually to provide alternatives or new policy ideas.

The dependence on commissioned projects inevitably leads to bias. Commissioned research will often defend and support a client's policies and not provide alternatives or criticisms. So it is that, with most regional think tank clients being governments, policy research generally supports and does not contest governmental policies. But before researchers can present their own visions and ideas regarding existing governmental policies, they need to be specialists with post-graduate degrees in the relevant areas of policy studies.

There are three basic criticisms of the current role of think tanks. First, their research supports government-related regional development projects. One of the many projects jointly financed by local government and the private sector in the late 1980s and early 1990s is the Seagaia resort in Miyazaki city, on the island of Kyushu in southern Japan. The Seagaia project, approved in 1989, was financed by a group including the Miyazaki prefectural government, Miyazaki city, and local businesses. The resort went bankrupt in February 2001. Although local government authorities made the final decisions to establish the resort and so are responsible for the results, it is think tanks that provided the research which defended the primary plans. Many joint projects that have failed reveal a similar lack of proper evaluation of both management and financial estimates by think tank research. As a result, authorities have often been required to reimburse the community, which has greatly depleted their budgets.

Second, the attitude of government staff toward think tanks is also a problem. If think tanks are to provide views and suggest policies that differ from those of the government, the authorities must consider the researchers to be equal partners or their counterparts, and should not ask the researchers to alter their analyses if they differ from or challenge government policy.

Third, the results of many commissioned projects are not available to the public, even though the projects are publicly sponsored. Given the centralized nature of policy development, often when specific issues have been discussed and analyzed by regional and local think tanks at the behest of central ministries, the research has been found to be a carbon copy of earlier reports with no plans suitable for a particular region or prefecture. If the quality of policy research is to improve, think tank research reports must be made public; after all, publicly financed research is not the concern solely of administrative bodies, but also of the public.

## REGIONAL POLICY COMPETITION

With the enactment of the Omnibus Law of Decentralization, Japan entered the era of policy decentralization, as a result of which regional policies are expected to change, bringing in their wake policy conflicts among local governments.

First, policy competition could become critical at the regional and local levels, with regional policymakers, local governments, and other regional actors fueling conflicts with other local authorities based on the fiscal potential and such other capacities as the management and policy-formulation ability of local governments. Although there was no competition among local governments while policymaking was centralized, there will henceforth be more policy divergence among local authorities (Sasaki 2000, 39–51). A case in point is the suggestion, by Tokyo Governor Ishihara Shintarō, of a new tax system whereby an asset-based corporate tax will be levied on major banks. This local tax is controversial, and the banks have sued the Tokyo government.[8]

Second, some of the new policy problems that have initially surfaced at the regional or local level are expected to spread nationwide. Although in centralized industrial societies social change generally first becomes apparent in urban areas, this, too, is changing in Japan; the aging population is now more apparent in rural villages, such as those in Iwate prefecture in the north, than in Tokyo. But, since the central government typically does not take the initiative to resolve emerging regional problems until they have spread nationwide, it cannot be expected to take immediate action regarding regional and local problems (Nihon Chihōjichi Kenkyūgakkai 1998, 7–9).

By contrast, in a decentralized society, problems are solved by policy actors, including citizens and local governments. They set up their own support systems for public policy research and establish innovative models in order to select the optimum regional policy processes.

## OPPORTUNITIES FOR REGIONAL THINK TANKS

In Japan, local authority is based on the principle of direct democracy. Governors and mayors are elected directly by voters in their constituencies, while political candidates advocate their political goals to the voters in election campaigns, and constituents select their leaders by comparing policy proposals. Think tanks, as public policy institutes, seem to function more efficiently and play an important role in the policy process where such direct democracy prevails, rather than under a system of indirect democracy, as is the case with the national government that is based on a parliamentary system. To date, policy proposals by outside actors, including think tanks, have been ignored in Japan's centralized system, with its powerful bureaucrats orchestrating the invisible and dominated policy process. The system is not designed to accept alternative ideas.

Lack of the legal requirement that information be disclosed has been one of the main reasons that think tanks have not played a significant role in the policy process. Local governments have compiled their own information disclosure rules and regulations, significantly ahead of the central ministries; to date all 47 prefectural and about 850 municipal governments have enacted information disclosure regulations. At the prefectural level, Kanagawa was the first to enact a disclosure ordinance in 1983, followed by the other prefectures, with Ehime finally enacting such a requirement in 1998. The central government's Freedom of Information Act was not enacted until April 2001. A pioneering disclosure ordinance was adopted by the Miyagi prefectural government in December 2000. Miyagi's Governor Asano Shirō debated and struggled with the prefectural police until the regulatory revision was finally enacted, marking the first time that the discretion and judgment of the Japanese police had been circumvented with regard to the disclosure of information.

The more transparent system will allow outside policy actors to play an ever-expanding role in the regional policy process. Given that regional issues differ significantly from those of the central government and are much closer to the community, the data necessary are more likely to be gathered than were the national political process involved. National policy issues are usually more complex, have more actors, and involve more diverse information that is harder to obtain.

## EXPANSION OF THINK TANK NETWORKS

While the expansion of these networks is essential if they are to be more influential and visible in the policy process, their policy research must be done by adequately skilled researchers and be made public. Several regional think tank networks are being established with a view to collaborating in the policy process, while in the global framework, networks such as the Global Development Network, Global ThinkNet, ASEAN-ISIS (Institutes for Strategic and International Studies), and Transition Policy Network are expanding (Struyk 2001).

The Think Tank Association of Japan, the largest network of regional policy institutions in the country, promotes research cooperation programs including annual conferences and forums, while several other networks, including both metropolitan and local government institutions, are also active.

Think tanks provide the opportunity for policy debates to be conducted, involving participants from various sectors and regions. As these networks and collaborative projects expand, so do the policy actors, which are increasingly including universities and local governments. For example, Policy Net—a network for policy analysts—was established in 1999, and has a diverse membership including policy researchers at universities and think tanks, administrative staff from the central government and local authorities, and members of the Diet and local assemblies. The institution, which seeks to advance policy research and ensure its effective use, holds an annual conference, the Policy Messe (http://www.policynet.jp).

Regional think tanks benefit from networks and information infrastructures since they permit the candid discussion of topics and the expression of independent views. The institutions, in turn, play an important role as alternate channels through which topics that government authorities find it difficult to tackle by initiating policy debates may be addressed. The networks are being expanded by think tanks that use information and communication technology (ICT) neworks and can tap organizational cooperative relationships.

## University-Affiliated Policy Institutes

Recently, a number of university-affiliated policy institutes have sought to join Japan's policy community. Limited though their policy-related activities have been to date, university-based researchers play an indispensable academic role in the policy process by participating in local government committees and councils. In addition to individual participation, university institutes are seeking to promote policy research by developing it as an academic discipline. Nevertheless, Japanese university institutes have rarely been recognized as think tanks or policy institutes because these institutions have been somewhat reluctant to apply their scholarly research to policy, and policy research has not been well developed as an academic discipline. University professors tend to focus their interest specifically and narrowly on their academic field and work within their academic circle.

In 1999, the Tokyo Metropolitan University's Center for Urban Studies, founded in 1977, became an interdisciplinary body for the study of urban issues. The center had decided to focus on policy research in 1994 and, within five years, became an independent body within the university and established new post-graduate courses in urban studies. The post-graduate education program has been broadened to train experts and professionals in the field of urban sciences; continuing education courses are available for those who are interested in urban policy—including local officials; and university-wide multidisciplinary policy research is being promoted using the center as an interface with all the university's researchers to promote policy studies. The purpose of serving as an interface is to enable research to be conducted to devise effective and useful policies for the Tokyo metropolitan government, the university's founder and sponsor. Moreover, since urban issues generally cover a wide range of subjects, analysis must reflect a multidisciplinary approach, while there must be interdisciplinary collaboration in the coordination of research.

Because the primary mission of the university institute is to advance academic interests, the center's professors and members frequently discuss the degree of their involvement in policy studies. These open discussions are useful in establishing a consensus on how best to advance policy research among university scholars and, together with members' endeavors, the center is expected to be a pioneering model of a Japanese university's policy research institute (http://www.comp .metro-u.ac.jp). University policy institutes are now seeking both to advance policy research academically, and to promote debate on regional and local policy processes.

The plan to privatize universities recently put forward by the national government has drawn attention to the role of publicly funded tertiary education. In addition to the role of university institutes in academic research and education, their regional contributions have become increasingly important. Such institutes already have an assured financial source, and with their distinguished research expertise, many are expected to play a leading role in the policy community. Compared with the existing Japanese think tanks, university institutes are able to maintain policy research autonomy without experiencing critical financial difficulty. Consequently, they are expected to promote policy evaluation, long-term historical policy studies, policy agenda setting, the detailed comparison of different policy ideas, and the promotion of multidisciplinary policy debates. In order to encourage more university institutes to participate in the policy process, policy research must be recognized as an academic pursuit. Moreover, universities have already established their independence, autonomy, and objectivity, and so their involvement in the policy process is expected.

## Community Think Tanks

Community-based think tanks are playing a leading role in policy decentralization, by pinpointing and solving policy problems in local communities. Staunchly defending regional independence and citizen sovereignty, these institutions can best be described as activity-oriented community think tanks that help citizens by providing opportunities to discuss policy issues with sufficient disclosure of information and exchange of information, and by establishing a sustainable community. Their principle is community development by the people, a concept that is completely different from the building and construction-based public works projects led by the civil service. Grass-roots community development involves the nurturing of a

sustainable community, helping the local citizens become autonomous and self-governing, as well as promoting regional revitalization,
a community outlook, and a cooperative community policy.

The main concern of these community think tanks is citizen participation and the policy process. Although citizens address many
problems through discussion with the local authorities, government
staff and members of local assemblies tackle most problems without
consulting the people or informing them about what is being done. But
by sharing information and providing alternatives and comparative
analyses, think tanks can help citizens solve their own problems.

In order to solve policy issues in the regional framework, think tank
researchers require expertise in the areas of networking and coordinating with a broad range of policy actors, including citizens, NPOs,
corporations, administrative officials, and specialists; communicating
and exchanging information with a variety of actors; planning and
designing decision-making frameworks according to which decisions
can be made regarding who to involve and how to discuss policy issues; and conducting research in and analysis of regional problems.

Community think tanks allow citizens' sovereignty to be tapped
and innovative policy ideas to be generated by the regional leadership.
They must, thus, broaden their expertise to include problem-solving
skills and innovation and, if they are to be more effective and influential
in the area of regional policy, a support system and a mechanism to
utilize regional resources to provide policy solutions should be devised
(NPO Seisaku Kenkyūsho 2000) based on the principles of regional
independence, citizen sovereignty, and a people/ information focus.

### Future Direction: A U.S. Example

In Japan, nonprofit regional think tanks are set up by prefectural governments and receive support from public organizations. It is inter-
esting to compare them with think tanks overseas, where they are run
along different lines. For example, the Public Policy Institute of California (PPIC), established in San Francisco in 1994, is dedicated to
improving public policy decision making in the state of California
through independent, objective, nonpartisan research. The PPIC was
established because it was generally recognized that the state lacked
"informed advice based upon adequate data and careful, objective

analysis," despite its being "one of the largest political and economic entities in the world." It was set up "to provide the State of California, particularly its elected representatives in the legislature and executive branch, with objective analysis of the major economic, social, and political issues facing the state" (Heynes 1993). PPIC produces independent policy research with its team of well-qualified academic scholars, and is quite different from the advocacy tanks that have recently sprung up among U.S. think tank institutes.

PPIC is financed mainly by project grants and earnings from a US$70 million William R. Hewlett endowment, that was established to lend a helping hand in recognition of the fund-raising pressure borne by public policy institutes and the risks faced by their staff when the nature of the activities in which they engage are dictated by the interest of funding sources. The endowment provides PPIC with the basic funding required to cover essential administrative functions and conduct pilot projects. The organization's research staff is appointed for a fixed number of years and is encouraged to network with the bureaucracy to ensure that important issues and PPIC policy suggestions are heeded.

The Economic Research Institute for Northeast Asia, a Japanese regional think tank, has an endowment of some ¥3,600 million. The endowment is financed by local authorities, government organizations, the business sector, and academic circles. The institute also received subsidies from the Niigata prefectural government. Another regional think tank, 21st Century Hyōgo Project Association, has an endowment of ¥2,600 million financed by business, the public sector, and academic circles. Although the endowments of these two institutes are substantial compared with those of other Japanese regional think tanks, they are small compared with PPIC's endowment. Perhaps Japan's think tank community might benefit from studying the structure of overseas think tanks such as PPIC.

## CONCLUSION

The Omnibus Law for Decentralization was enacted as a result of a movement that demanded increased political leadership as well as greater pluralism in the policy process. There is thus a need, if greater policy decentralization is to be achieved, for the relationship among government authorities as well as the entire policymaking system to be changed to a horizontal, cooperative system from a vertically controlled and coercive one.

In the interests of achieving a decentralized society, grass-roots involvement should be encouraged in developing and sustaining public interest and the regional infrastructure. But, in order for government bodies to relinquish some of their policymaking activities, they must first change their attitude to external policy actors, including think tanks, and help create a policy infrastructure and support system. This would allow—as in civil society in other countries—a variety of policy advocacy groups to propose policy ideas and policies to be selected and implemented in cooperation with a variety of actors, including elected officials, government authorities, and constituents. And, where such competitive democratic policy processes are at work, think tanks play a major role.

To simultaneously achieve policy decentralization and advance pluralism, regional policy infrastructures must first be developed to meet local needs. To this end, consideration must be given to the development of financial resources, including funds for policy research; the disclosure and utilization of think tank research; setting up cooperative relationships with universities; and expanding think tank networks. While the majority of regional think tanks are currently connected to and often controlled by local administrative bodies, they could in future be transformed to resemble those institutes set up since the introduction of the NPO Law; political or advocacy think tanks that, for example, assist governors or local assemblies; or public-focused civic institutions.

It is time that the role of think tanks as public policy institutes be reconsidered. Public policy research can no longer continue to be limited to the narrow consulting requirements of companies or industries, and it must be recognized that bureaucrats involved in the policy process cannot be unbiased and propose long-term strategies or ideas that might produce a drastic change or paradigm shift. Think tanks, on the other hand, can tackle diverse issues with a multidisciplinary approach, and design and propose new or alternative policy goals, which serve to deepen policy discussions. They should have their own policy experts, schooled in various disciplines, not researchers seconded from administrative bodies who cannot be completely unbiased regarding existing policies.

Think tanks are well placed to promote the discussion of policy issues and so can play a leading role in advancing political leadership and civil sovereignty to enhance the country's system of governance. In this era of policy decentralization, regional think tanks can be expected to become more effective and influential as they become increasingly involved in the policy process.

## NOTES

1. Dickson (1971) refers to "Mother RAND" in his book, which is one of the early publications on think tanks.

2. The six institutes are the Hamburg Institute for Economic Research (HWWA, founded in 1908), the Kiel Institute of World Economics (IfW, 1914), the German Institute for Economic Research (DIW, 1925), the Rhein-Westphalia Institute for Economic Research (RWI, 1943), the Ifo Institute for Economic Research (Ifo, 1949), and the Halle Institute for Economic Research (IWH, 1992.). All six institutes appear on the blue list; the Hamburg and Kiel institutes are public institutions, and the other four are NPOs.

3. Such dilemmas include the ruling elite and pluralist models.

4. Nevertheless, the concentration is on Tokyo's problems as 54 percent of think tank institutes and 79 percent of all researchers are located in the Tokyo metropolitan area.

5. Yamaichi Securities, one of Japan's four top security companies, went bankrupt and closed down in June 1999.

6. The LTCB was acquired by an investment group comprising Ripplewood Holdings and other investors. It was renamed the Shinsei Bank in June 2000.

7. Hokkaido Takushoku Bank, established in 1900, was the first city bank to declare bankruptcy, which it did in November 1997. Its branches in Hokkaido were taken over by North Pacific Bank and those on Japan's main island of Honshu by Chūō Trust and Banking.

8. Details of the new tax are discussed in chapter 6.

## BIBLIOGRAPHY

Dickson, Paul. 1971. *Think Tanks*. New York: Atheneum.
Durning, Dan. 1993. "Participatory Policy Analysis in a Social Service Agency:

A Case Study." *Journal of Policy Analysis and Management* 12(2): 297–322.

Gellner, Winand. 1998. "Think Tanks in Germany." In Diane Stone et al., eds. *Think Tanks Across Nations—A Comparative Approach.* Manchester, U.K.: Manchester University Press.

Heynes, Roger. 1993. Unpublished concept paper for the Public Policy Institute of California.

Katagata Zenji. 1970. *Shinku tanku* (Think tanks). Tokyo: Nihon Seisansei Honbu.

Kyushu Economic Research Center. 2000. *Kyūshū keizai hakusho 2000* (Economic survey of Kyushu 2000). Fukuoka, Japan: Kyushu Economic Research Center.

McGann, James G., and R. Kent Weaver, eds. 2000. *Think Tanks & Civil Societies—Catalysts for Ideas and Action.* New Brunswick, N.J.: Transaction Publishers.

Ministry of International Trade and Industry. 1971. *Nihon no shinku tanku* (Think tanks in Japan). Tokyo: Diamond Inc.

Miyakawa Tadao. 1995. *Seisaku kagaku nyūmon* (An introduction to policy science). Tokyo: Toyo Keizai Shinpōsha.

———. 2000. "The Role of Policy Analysis for Democratic Policy-Making." *NIRA Review* (Winter): 10–13. <http://www.nira.go.jp/publ/review/2000winter/index.hjtml> (July 2001).

National Institute for Research Advancement. 1997. "Shinku tanku" (Think tanks). *NIRA Seisaku Kenkyū* 10(6): 1–61.

———. 1999. *NIRA's World Directory of Think Tanks 1999.* Tokyo: National Institute for Research Advancement.

———. 2000. *Shinku tanku yōran 2000* (Directory of think tanks in Japan 2000). Tokyo: National Institute for Research Advancement.

Nihon Chihōjichi Kenkyūgakkai. 1998. *Chihōjichi no sentan riron* (New theoretical analysis of local autonomy). Tokyo: Keisō Shobō.

NPO Seisaku Kenkyūsho. 2000. *Komyuniti shinku tanku no susume: Chiiki no mondai kaiketsuryoku wo sapōto suru tame ni* (Encouraging community think tanks—supporting their regional resolution-finding ability). Nara, Japan: NPO Seisaku Kenkyūsho.

Ōya Minoru, Ōta Shin'ichi, and Mayama Tatsushi, ed. 1998. Sōgō seisaku kagaku nyūmon (Guide to general policy science). Tokyo: Seibundō.

Rich, Andrew. 2000. "The Characteristics and Influence of State Think Tanks." Interim Report to the Public Policy Institute of California. Unpublished.

Sasaki Nobuo. 2000. *Jichitai no kōkyō seisaku nyūmon* (Guide to local governmental policy research). Tokyo: Gyōsei.

Stone, Diane. 1996. *Capturing Political Imagination—Think Tanks and the Policy Process.* London: Frank Cass.

Struyk, Raymond J. 2001. *Management of Transnational Think Tank Networks.* (unpublished).

# 6 Prospects for a Self-Sustainable Local Fiscal System

## Numao Namiko

This chapter considers the financial problems currently facing local governments from the perspective of their root cause: the state of intergovernmental fiscal relations and the fiscal policy mix of the 1990s. Local governments' finances are in starkly worse shape than is, perhaps, generally recognized: Long-term central government debt is putting pressure on local governments' finances. This chapter investigates measures with which local governments will overcome financial crisis and further establish independence from the central government.

## THE STRUCTURE OF LOCAL FINANCES

Together, local governments derive some 35 percent of their revenues from local taxes, with another 50 percent coming from grants, subsidies, and local bond issues (table 1). When the figure is broken down, one finds that the 47 prefectures secure more than half their tax revenue from inhabitant and enterprise taxes, which are unstable sources,

Table 1. Revenue Structure of Local Public Finance (¥100 mn, %)

| | FY1998 | | FY1999 | | Fluctuation | |
|---|---|---|---|---|---|---|
| | Revenue Accounts | Per-centage | Revenue Accounts | Per-centage | Revenue Accounts | Per-centage |
| Local Tax (1) | 359,222 | 34.9 | 350,261 | 33.7 | –8,961 | –2.5 |
| Inhabitant tax | 89,584 | 8.7 | 87,671 | 8.4 | –1,913 | –2.1 |
| Corporate and en-terprise tax | 73,604 | 7.2 | 65,285 | 6.3 | –8,319 | –11.3 |
| Consumption tax | 25,504 | 2.5 | 24,793 | 2.4 | –711 | –2.8 |
| Other taxes | 170,530 | 16.6 | 172,512 | 16.6 | 1,982 | 1.2 |
| Local transfer tax (2) | 5,952 | 0.6 | 6,089 | 0.6 | 137 | 2.3 |
| Local exceptional transfer (3) | – | – | 6,399 | 0.6 | – | – |
| Local Allocation Tax (4) | 180,489 | 17.5 | 208,642 | 20.1 | 28,153 | 15.6 |
| National treasury dis-bursements | 157,451 | 15.3 | 165,990 | 16.0 | 8,539 | 5.4 |
| Disbursement for Public Works | 63,039 | 6.1 | 61,068 | 5.9 | –1,971 | –3.1 |
| Local bond issues | 151,356 | 14.7 | 130,733 | 12.6 | –20,623 | –13.6 |
| Others | 174,219 | 17.0 | 171,951 | 16.5 | –2,268 | –1.3 |
| Total | 1,028,689 | 100 | 1,040,065 | 100 | –11,376 | 1.1 |
| Ordinary expendi-ture = (1) + (2) + (3) + (4) | 545,663 | 53.0 | 571,391 | 54.9 | 25,728 | 4.7 |

Source: Ministry of Public Management, Home Affairs, Posts and Telecommunications (2001b).

Note: The category of disbursement known as local exceptional transfer was created in fiscal 1999 (ended March 31, 2000).

particularly given the current economic situation. Meanwhile, some 3,200 municipalities, towns, and villages derive most of their tax revenue from inhabitant, fixed asset, and local consumption taxes.[1] But local governments are beholden to the central government for their tax revenues by virtue of the Local Tax Law, which regulates the standard tax rate and the limited tax rate.

There are two main types of fiscal transfer from the center to local governments. One takes the form of the Local Allocation Tax, which is distributed according to established revenues and needs. It comprises a set proportion of the five national taxes—32 percent of income and alcohol, 35.8 percent of corporate, 29.5 percent of consumption, and 25 percent of tobacco tax—which is designated as local revenues and allocated according to an established formula designed to redress the differences in local tax revenues and allow freedom of local administration.

The second type of transfer comprises specific subsidies called national treasury disbursements that are divided into three categories: payments for the central government's subcontract functions, such as national elections; payments for specific tasks for which the central government is responsible as provided by the Local Government Finance Act, such as those that support welfare benefits and compulsory education; and grants-in-aid to allow implementation of policies that the central government supports, encourages, or promotes.

These revenue transfers from the central government represent more than 50 percent of the local governments' total revenues (fig. 1), without which they would find it very difficult to supply the services required by society. In other words, built into the structure of local public finance is a dependence on the central government. Funds transferred to local governments from national coffers constitute about two-thirds of all local-government expenditures. With these sources of revenue, local governments supply various public services, such as the police, education, social welfare, and public works.

During the high-growth period of the 1960s until the mid-1970s, revenue transfers ensured that public services would be of a uniform standard nationwide, even in small towns and villages where the local tax revenue represented less than 10 percent of the total revenue. However, since the mid-1980s, when the central government began to undertake fiscal reconstruction, it has been a struggle to keep up the revenue transfers, which has forced the central government to begin seeking ways to ensure local governments' revenue.

## Financial Crisis of Local Government

The serious fiscal crisis confronting many of Japan's local governments became evident in the 1990s. Because of decline in central government subsidies, local tax cuts, and a decrease in local tax revenue, a growing shortage threatened local finance. While some relief came from municipal bonds and loans extended from the Local Allocation Tax special account, the cumulative debt of local governments continued to increase so that, at the end of fiscal year 2001 (ended March 31, 2002), local governments' unpaid loans were expected to total ¥187 trillion. The interest on this figure amounts to about 14 percent of all local governments' yearly budgets. As a result, ordinary expenditures—such as outlays for personnel, social assistance, and local

**Figure 1.** National and Local Government Expenditure

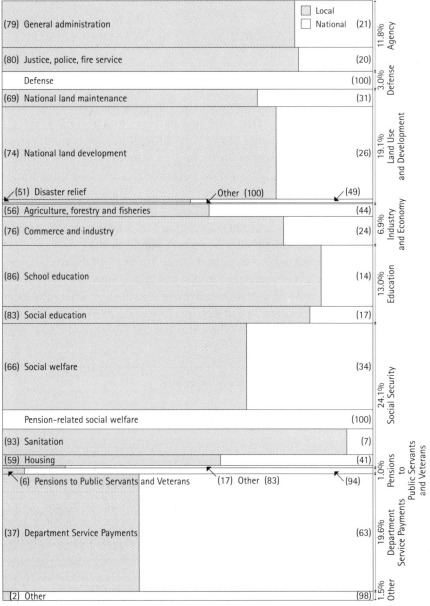

*Source:* Ministry of Public Management, Home Affairs, Posts and Telecommunications (2001b).

*Note:* Numbers in parentheses are percentages.

loans—represent some 87.5 percent of their total ordinary general revenue. Just in fiscal year 1999 (ended March 31, 2000), more than 60 percent of all local governments were saddled with a debt-expenditure ratio of at least 15 percent.

Behind the local government fiscal crisis lie three major factors: increased expenditures for the social security of a graying population; local spending policies in the wake of the tax cuts following the 1990s collapse of the bubble economy; and lax management of funds received from the central government through revenue transfers. In other words, even though the tax revenue has been decreasing annually, local expenditure has been expanding, particularly in the area of social capital and social aid.

## Fiscal Relations between the Central and Local Governments

Certainly the fiscal problems of local governments have been compounded by lax management on their part and the decline of tax revenues, due to the prolonged recession. Nevertheless, the situation has been exacerbated by the degree to which local governments' authority vis-à-vis their fiscal affairs has been circumscribed, and the structure and operation of their finances are affected by the policies of the central government.

In comparison with other major industrial nations, Japan's fiscal policy at the local government level is characterized by an unusually high ration of spending to revenues and authority (Jinno and Kaneko 1998). While Japan has a unitary rather than federal form of government, local governments provide 60 percent to 70 percent of the services. And, given their lack of fiscal autonomy, it might well be said that prefectures and municipalities function more like local branches of the central government than as autonomous fiscal bodies.

In areas of public finance such as resource allocation, income redistribution, and macroeconomic stabilization, central and local governments operate under a unified system, with the central government guaranteeing the revenues required to provide a uniform level of government services and public goods nationwide, thereby redistributing income among the regions and leveling out economic performance. Andrew DeWit (2000) notes that, unlike in the United States, where the leveling of the progressive structure of income taxes and the hiking of the minimum tax level since the 1980s have resulted in a major backlash from those in lower income brackets, there is no highly visible conflict between the different income groups in Japan. Bearing in mind the structure of local government finances and the Local Allocation Tax, he argues that Japan's system of income redistribution places greater store on interregional rather than interpersonal transfers. However, this system of unified income distribution has ceased to function properly and is replete with problems. In its wake have developed three overarching factors that have contributed to the crisis in local government finances: the impact of tax cuts, the transfer of operational authority from the center, and the redirection of local government spending to counter the recession. These are dealt with in turn below.

THE IMPACT OF TAX CUTS    Japan's local government revenue structure is weak and unstable. The balance between local spending and local revenues is heavily skewed toward the former: While conducting some 70 percent of central and local government operations, local governments collect only about 40 percent of the taxes. Furthermore, even local governments' autonomy in imposing taxes is limited: They need central government agreement to adjust tax rates beyond predefined parameters and introduce new taxes.

In addition, local taxation is deficient in terms of proportionality to benefits, burden sharing, stability, and universality. The main taxes at the prefectural level are the inhabitant and enterprise taxes, both of which are linked to the central government's corporate tax, assessed on the basis of corporate income. The amounts collected vary considerably depending on the state of the economy,[2] and as a result may cause severe financial instability. Regardless of the state of the economy, prefectures face essential outlays—such as the payment of police and public school teachers' salaries—and can ill afford to lose revenue when a prolonged recession hits or the central government cuts its tax rates.

At the municipal level, the fixed asset tax and inhabitant tax are the revenue mainstays. But since the latter is assessed according to the amount of taxable income as determined by the national income tax, any increase the central government might make in deductions to lower the income tax burden automatically causes municipal revenues to decline.

During the 1990s, local governments saw their revenues slip steadily as a result of the long recession following the bursting of the economic bubble, and this tendency was aggravated by the effects of counter-cyclical tax cuts by the central government. Every year from fiscal 1994 (ended March 31, 1995), the central government has implemented tax reductions to fight the recession, causing local revenues to decline further. In fiscal 1999, the central government introduced permanent reductions in income and corporate taxes, and lowered the maximum rate for the inhabitant tax and the basic enterprise tax rate, thereby reducing the local governments' revenues from the local inhabitant and enterprise taxes.

To offset the impact of these reductions, the central government transferred a portion of its revenues from the tobacco tax to the local governments, set up a new system of supplementary grants, and increased the percentage of the corporate tax distributed to the Local Allocation Tax designated for local governments. However, these were stopgap measures, designed to balance the books for that fiscal year, and were not consistent with the principles of proportionality to benefits, burden sharing, and stability in local taxation.

To date, local governments lack the authority to make decisions concerning the taxes that provide their fundamental sources of revenue, and the central government continues to use them as tools for its recession-fighting economic policies.

TRANSFER OF OPERATIONAL AUTHORITY FROM THE CENTRAL GOVERNMENT    A second factor that has contributed to the crisis in local government finances is the cutting back of central government subsidies in the latter part of the 1980s. Previously, when a local government had undertaken social welfare– or social capital–related projects, the amount by which subsidies might have been curtailed had been included in the estimate of local needs to be covered by the Local Allocation Tax. However, as local fiscal demand gradually increased, the total amount could not be secured through this system due to the ceiling on local or central government revenue transfers. To cover the shortfall, the Local Allocation Tax special account thus took out a loan, the principal and interest payments on which were split equally between the central and local governments.

But this was no long-term solution, as can be seen from the example of how the old-age welfare system was affected. For many years, the Welfare Law for the Elderly had required that the state assist the elderly in need. But, with the graying of the population and the increase in the number of nuclear, rather than extended, families, nursing care for the elderly had shifted from a system designed to assist needy individuals to one provided as a universal service. As the nature of the service changed, demands became more diverse and it was gradually felt that municipalities, being the level of government closest to residents, were best suited to providing the relevant services.

Thus, in the latter part of the 1980s, the concept of decentralization was taken up as a key direction for welfare reform and, in 1993, a major reform was undertaken: The authority over admission to old-age welfare facilities was transferred from prefectures to towns and villages. In addition, starting in 1993, municipalities were required to draw up old-age health and welfare plans and to survey the local demand for old-age services, based on which they had to draw up a plan for provision of these services and submit progress reports.

The decentralization of welfare administration was partly related to the central government's financial difficulties, as a result of which a move began in 1985 to reduce national treasury disbursements. In 1986, the subsidies for local spending on health care and welfare at facilities for the elderly was slashed to 50 percent of the total costs of projects. Moreover, when responsibility for institutionalized care of the elderly in towns and villages was shifted from the prefectural to the town and village level, it was decided that the cost burden which had previously been equally shared by the national government and the prefectures was to be covered by the national government, prefectures, as well as towns and villages in the ration of 2:1:1.

The municipalities, towns, and villages had to cover the additional fiscal burden out of their general revenues, but, according to a study by Takeda Hiroshi (1995), special supplementary payments under the Local Allocation Tax compensated for only about 20 percent of the increase. This was because, for example, the central government modified the basis according to which the Local Allocation Tax payments for welfare services for the elderly were calculated by replacing some veteran employees with lower-paid workers so the overall level of Local Allocation Tax payments could be held down. In sum, the provision of revenues to cover the additional fiscal burden resulting from the decentralization of these government operations was insufficient.

LOCAL GOVERNMENT SPENDING TO FIGHT THE RECESSION    The efficiency with which local governments have been introducing public works based on national programs is also, by hindsight, a cause of their fiscal crisis.

Local governments have vigorously promoted public works, such as the construction of roads, bridges, and sewers, partly as business-stimulating measures. Compared to other Organization for Economic Co-operation and Development (OECD) countries, Japan is the only country in which expenditure for social infrastructure has not, since the 1980s, decreased as a percentage of gross domestic product (GDP). Whereas in most OECD countries social infrastructure expenditure at the local level runs at 2 percent to 3 percent of GDP, it remains at the high level of 7 percent to 8 percent in Japan.

The reason can be traced to the period immediately after World War II, when there was an urgent need to build up the country's social infrastructure, to which end Japan's local governments were brought into play to ensure the well-balanced restructuring of the country's postwar economy. This system of public works development thrived no less as local economies began to falter with the collapse of agriculture, because regional incomes thus became increasingly dependent on the subsidies received from the central government for public works performed based on a central government plan. It was precisely through this local public works spending that the central government sought to fight the recession. However, the economic situation has changed so much that to do so now would mean certain financial ruin for local governments.

Currently, the financial picture at the prefectural level is extremely bleak, particularly in major metropolitan areas such as Tokyo and Osaka, which have devoted an especially high percentage of ordinary revenue to ordinary expenses. These two areas have been hit harder than others for two principal reasons: corporate and other tax revenues have decreased as a result of the prolonged recession; and the high cost of interest and principal payments on bonds issued for major public works projects during the bubble years, besides which they have the added burden of having to maintain these facilities.

At the municipal level, the scene is no different. In addition to the increased cost of providing welfare services for an aging population, the burden of outlays for basic infrastructure, such as roads and sewer systems, has been a major underlying factor contributing to the financial crisis. Municipalities are bearing heavy costs for both servicing the debt incurred by the bonds issued to finance the construction, and maintaining this infrastructure.

How did this situation come about? During the 1989–1990 Japan-U.S. Structural Impediments Initiative (SII) talks, Washington insisted that the Japanese government raise the level of public investment in order to eliminate the surplus of savings over investment, which it identified as the cause of Japan's persistent tendency to export more than it imports. Because the United States feared that public investment aimed at improving the infrastructure for manufacturing would cause Japan's productivity to increase further and thereby make its trade surplus with the United States even bigger, Washington expected Tokyo to concentrate the increase in the area of quality-of-life investments in social overhead capital.

In 1991, Tokyo announced a ¥430 trillion Basic Plan for Public Investment covering the decade through fiscal 2000 (ended March 31, 2001), and in fiscal 1995 (ended on March 31, 1996) the total was increased to ¥630 trillion; this plan included projects—such as roads, sewage systems, waste treatment plants, and urban parks—to be implemented by local governments either independently or partly with subsidies from the central government. The Local Allocation Tax was used as one of the revenue sources.[3]

Essentially, the Local Allocation Tax is a system of vertical and horizontal revenue transfers. A certain portion of the national tax receipts is moved vertically to the Local Allocation Tax special account for distribution, horizontally, to local governments according to their estimated standard tax revenue and financial needs. Although the fiscal requirements of each local government are calculated according to population and area, should a local government be undertaking a project being promoted by the central government, that project would come under the heading of estimated fiscal needs, and the local government in question would receive more revenue to cover those costs. Similarly, should projects the central government encourages be financed by floating local bonds, the central government would take both the expense and the cost of redeeming the bonds into consideration when estimating the Local Allocation Tax.

In 1992, the government began adopting a variety of stimulus measures, including those requiring additional public investment by local governments. Of the ¥100 trillion available in antirecessionary public investment, about ¥20 trillion was assigned to local governments. Then, in the late 1990s, the central government encouraged expenditure for public works by local governments by paying part of their costs through national disbursements or the Local Allocation Tax, and encouraging the flotation of local debt.

A local administrative official reported at that time: "The role of the Local Allocation Tax is changing. We can get more grants for certain projects for local needs. The more projects we do, the more grants we can get. This is local competition, and we are doing our best to win the race and get more grants and subsidies."[4] But most of the many local governments that utilized this system found their finances increasingly burdened by expenditures for public bonds and the maintenance of facilities constructed as public works projects.

Originally, the guarantee of revenues to local governments on the basis of the central government's blueprint for local finances was seen as an assurance of a national minimum level of public services regardless of regional economic strength or fiscal resources. But after the mid-1980s, when the basic social infrastructure was in place, the central government urged local governments to carry out public works projects that would meet local needs, as a result of which not a few governments built up their social infrastructure through bond flotations and the Local Allocation Tax. As the recession dragged on and the fiscal situation became critical, however, the national government became unable to provide the revenue to support local governments and borrowed increasingly through the Local Allocation Tax special account, which caused the volume of outstanding local government bonds to balloon.[5] In fiscal year 2000, the debt borne by the special account totaled ¥34 trillion.

Thus, the Ministry of Finance and the Ministry of Public Management, Home Affairs, Posts and Telecommunications both recently agreed on appropriate measures to deal with this shortfall in local finance: Loans from the Local Allocation Tax special account will not be increased, while the central government will periodically reconsider its revenue disbursements to local governments with a view to making up shortfall in local funds. But despite the agreement, the ministries appear still to be deliberating how best to proceed.

Another area feeling the brunt of the recessions is the local third sector, set up in the 1980s to develop recreational facilities. Some, saddled with huge debts, have failed. Although the local governments are the guarantors of their loans and so bear the liability when third-sector developments fail, it has been increasingly difficult for the central government to make up for the local shortfalls due to decreasing tax revenues and increasing expenditures for public bonds.

## REFORM OF LOCAL GOVERNMENT FINANCES

Now that the central government has reached the limit of its ability to guarantee local government revenues, what sort of reforms are being sought to overcome the crisis in local public finances? Here we will consider and compare the reform proposals of the Committee for the Promotion of Decentralization and the Council on Economic and Fiscal Policy.

### Committee for the Promotion of Decentralization

Under the 1995 Law for Promotion of Decentralization, the Committee for the Promotion of Decentralization was set up as an advisory organ reporting to the prime minister. The committee focused its attention mainly on the issues of eliminating intervention and regulation by the central government, and transferring revenue sources to local governments in order to avoid the evils of excessive centralization of power. Local governments were already handling many of the public sector's operations, but they did not have the authority to conduct these activities autonomously.

In its first set of recommendations, issued in December 1996, the Committee for the Promotion of Decentralization called for local governments to have broad responsibility for the conduct of administration in the regions on an independent, comprehensive basis, with the operations of the central government to be limited to: (1) operations involving Japan's existence as a state within the international community, (2) operations involving public activities better decided on a uniform basis at the national level, or basic rules concerning local self-government, and (3) measures and projects needing to be implemented on a nationwide scale or from a nationwide perspective.

In addition, as an exceptional category within the overall field of operations for which the central government is ultimately responsible, the council proposed the designation of both statutory delegated operations (those better entrusted to local governments for reasons of public convenience or administrative efficiency) and directly controlled operations (those directed by the central government).

In its second set of recommendations, the committee set forth proposals for the fiscal arrangements to accompany this new division of operational responsibilities. Initially, the committee came out with proposals that stuck to the concept of Article 9 of the Local Government Finance Act, which calls for local governments to pay the entire cost of the activities for which they are responsible. The committee's goal was to clarify the autonomy and responsibility of local governments in handling their own affairs, and to lessen the central government's involvement in and control over local government affairs through the consolidation and elimination of subsidies from the national treasury.

The committee sought to create a system whereby local governments would carry out their own operations on their own responsibility by maximizing the scope of autonomous activities funded by independent revenue sources; to this end it called for payments from the national treasury to be severely limited and for subsidized activities to be reduced. The committee also called for expansion of local governments' independent revenue through the transfer of tax sources from the central government, for elimination of the restrictions on local tax rates, and for a system respecting the autonomous decisions of local governments in connection with bond issues through the elimination of the requirement for central government approval. In addition, the recommendations included a call for increased transfers of revenues under the Local Allocation Tax to guarantee revenues for those regions where local tax revenues could not be relied on because of such factors as depopulation.

But the committee ran into broad resistance from bureaucratic organs with respect to a number of its concepts, as a result of which it did not include many specific points in its formal recommendations. It did not make a single specific recommendation concerning the transfer of tax sources, and with respect to the consolidation and elimination of subsidies it offered concrete ideas only for a limited number of operations. The committee's proposals produced certain results, such as the elimination of the approval requirement for the creation of new local taxes and for local bond issues, but these have been utilized as a tool to promote the principle of local fiscal responsibility without the transfer of revenue sources.

The Committee for the Promotion of Decentralization disbanded in May 2001, but even in its final set of recommendations it noted the importance of transferring both operational authority and control of revenue sources to local governments, and urged the establishment of the principle of local responsibility based on local authority.

### Council on Economic and Fiscal Policy

In June 2001, the government's Council on Economic and Fiscal Policy issued a set of recommendations titled "Structural Reform of the Japanese Economy: Basic Policies for Macroeconomic Management," which are often referred to as the solidly built (*honebuto*) reform policies. The council's basic position was one that stressed the need for an economy based on autonomy and self-reliance; in the area of local affairs, it called for a switch from the traditional approach of uniform, nationwide development to one that emphasizes the distinctive features of each region and that invigorates the regions through competition among them.

However, as the first step toward achieving regional autonomy, the council set forth the policy direction of merging municipalities into larger units from the perspective of the need for a stronger base of local administration. Second, in order to allow local governments to exercise independent judgment, the council adopted the basic principle that authority over administrative services should be exercised at a level close to residents, calling for the reduction of involvement by the central government in local affairs and for the rebuilding of local government finances from the perspective of achieving greater efficiency in the use of public funds and clarifying benefits and burdens. To this end, the council proposed (1) reduction of subsidies and other payments from the national treasury, (2) review of the Local Allocation Tax, and (3) strengthening of local revenue sources.

In terms of the prescription for curing the crisis in local finances, the recommendations of this council look very similar to the vision of decentralized public administration and finances set forth by the Committee for the Promotion of Decentralization. However, the two bodies had different underlying philosophies.

The traditional system of local government in Japan was one in which all the local authorities had to do was follow the instructions they received from the central government and they would feel virtually no pain in covering the costs of social infrastructure projects, although this produced a break in the connection between benefits and burdens at the local level, causing local residents to develop a distorted view of fiscal affairs, which in turn led to lax management of local government finances.

The Council on Economic and Fiscal Policy thus adopted the position that, in order to cut out wasteful spending, the national subsidies and Local Allocation Tax should be reformed so as to achieve maximum congruence between benefits and burdens at the local level. In addition, since the large numbers of small municipalities meant duplication of facilities and other unnecessary costs, the council called for the construction of an efficient system of local administration through the amalgamation of municipalities into larger units with populations of 200,000 and 300,000 people, the level that empirical studies have shown to be the most efficient.

The council adopted a consistent position of following the principle of paying one's own way at the local level, both in economic and fiscal affairs. But it did not take up the issue of reviewing the division of functions between the central and local governments. Also, its main focus was on addressing the problems in the finances of the central government, and for this reason it proposed cutting back on transfers of revenues to local governments and having them work harder at raising their own funds. The thinking behind this was that, were the subsidies and Local Allocation Tax payments from the central government cut successively because the central government was in a financial crisis, the situation at the local level, where the base of revenue sources is weak, would be even more critical.

The discussion of reform of local government finances is now being directed less at the issue of how revenue sources should be divided between the center and the regions, and more at the search for ways to have local governments bear fiscal burdens based on the principle of self-accountability. In the following section we will review the direction of the reforms being proposed.

## FINANCIAL REFORMS IN
## THE INTERESTS OF LOCAL INDEPENDENCE

Reform of the local government system under the Omnibus Law of Decentralization started in April 2000. However, reform on the fiscal level has been slow, with the transfer from center to local governments of decisions regarding the tax base having been held off for future discussion. While the introduction of radical taxation reform may well take time, it is imperative that a degree of reform be immediately instituted in several areas as outlined below.

### The Local Allocation Tax

In recent years, it has been argued that the Local Allocation Tax should be reduced in scale because it clouds the relationship between benefits and burdens, thereby promoting laxness in the management of local government finances. But if the scale of this revenue-sharing system is reduced without other arrangements being changed, it can be expected that even greater financial difficulties will face local governments, particularly in those regions where the potential tax base is small.

The Ministry of Public Management, Home Affairs, Posts and

Telecommunications is now working on reforming the Local Allocation Tax, with the focus on the current methods of adjusting the
amounts in line with the circumstances of individual local governments.[6] One of the items to be revised is the system of second subsidies,
namely, those payments supplementing the regular local allocation tax
that account for 40 percent of the second subsidies as calculated by
methods of adjusting the amounts.[7] These subsidies distort the fiscal
adjustment function of the Local Allocation Tax, for which reason
there have been calls for their review for some time.

A second item due for revision is the method of adjustment according to which more generous payments are provided to local jurisdictions with smaller populations, based on the view that their per-capita
costs tend to be higher. The central government had already revised
this system, adapting the uniform modification coefficient when cal-
culating the specific needs of a depopulated district for the purposes
of the Local Allocation Tax for municipalities with a population of less
than 4,000. As a result, some of these small local governments are
obliged to amalgamate because they cannot make financial ends meet
on such meager subsidies.

Local Allocation Tax reforms are under way starting with the reduction of the supplementary portion for low-population municipalities. Given the ballooning of the special account for this system,
however, we are likely to see calls emerging for a reduction of the total
amount paid. Yet, if local governments assume responsibility for more
operations, the gaps among the regions will naturally widen, and the
role of the Local Allocation Tax in smoothing the differences will become even more important.

### The Local Tax Base

If one takes the position that revenue sources should be apportioned
between the center and the regions in a way that matches the division
of operational responsibilities in order for local governments to be
able to exercise autonomous decision-making authority, then it follows both that local governments must secure their own revenue
sources and that a clear relationship between benefits and burdens
must be established at the local level. As a way of achieving this, it has
been proposed that the existing tax system be reformed so that, among

other things, the main taxes might be transferred from the center to the regions.

The main taxes in question are the income and consumption taxes. A typical suggestion involving income tax calls for the transfer of an amount, corresponding to the minimum tax rate (10 percent) to local governments as an inhabitant tax (Jinno and Kaneko 1998). One of the suggestions concerning the consumption tax (currently 5 percent, of which 1 percent goes to local governments), meanwhile, calls for modification of the existing apportionment of revenues between the center and local governments.

Proposals have also been advanced for reform of the existing local tax system. One plan calls for changing the corporate enterprise tax assessed by prefectures from a tax on corporate income (linked to the corporate tax at the national level) to one on operations (as measured by the size of the business). Since even corporations reporting losses in their financial statements are the beneficiaries of certain public services, it would seem only reasonable to have them, too, share the burden. At present, two thirds of all corporations are running deficits, meaning that they are paying no corporate income tax.

In July 1997, a subcommittee of the government's Tax Commission came up with four proposals to change the method of assessing the enterprise tax, the simplest of which would be to assess taxes on the basis of the amount of capital, although doing so on the basis of the value added from production is much more appropriate. Discussions have, however, come to a halt and shall have to be resumed before any proposal can be implemented. Meanwhile, small and medium-sized enterprises in the red have been getting special tax breaks, but there have been calls for these to be replaced with subsidies or other forms of income transfer.

## Taxation Exceeding Standard Tax Rates

The Local Tax Law regulates the kind of local taxes, the tax base, and the tax rate. When there are special fiscal needs, such as to finance public works, the imposition of a tax at other than the standard rate is allowed, but permission from the Ministry of Public Management, Home Affairs, Posts and Telecommunications is required.

However, the central government makes it difficult for local governments to assess taxes to cover basic fiscal needs on the grounds that the latter have already been compensated by the Local Allocation Tax. Moreover, tax cuts aimed at stimulating business are not allowable.

Adopting tax rates that exceed the standard rate is an effective way of raising funds to meet special local needs, so currently almost all prefectures are adding surcharges to their corporate inhabitant taxes, while municipalities are doing so to inhabitant taxes and fixed assets taxes. Bearing this in mind, it would seem worth considering giving local governments more leeway in applying tax rates that exceed the standard rate to cover ordinary expenses and achieve policy objectives.

## Local Discretionary Taxes

Since April 2000, local governments have been allowed to impose discretionary taxes after consulting—rather than seeking permission from—the central government, so that each local government is now able to construct its own earmarked tax in addition to the ordinary tax. Another change since the start of fiscal 2000 concerns the requirements to be fulfilled for the tax to be applied. The tax had to satisfy five requirements, two of these—related to tax resources and fiscal needs —have been eliminated leaving three, namely: that the tax base should not be the same as the national tax or other local taxes, and the tax burden should not become too heavy; that the tax should not pose serious damage in physical distribution; and that the tax must be appropriate to national economic policy. So now, even in the absence of special fiscal needs, local governments are able to construct their own tax and, since applications of the revenue from the earmarked tax are possible, the relation between benefits and burdens is clear.

Be that as it may, local governments remain subject to constraints in terms of their ability to impose discretionary taxes, and in practice it is difficult for them to introduce such taxes as a means of raising general revenues. Thus, we are now seeing moves in various places to create new taxes either to supplement existing tax systems or to achieve specific policy objectives.

These new taxes can be classified into three categories. The first comprises environment-related taxes. These are imposed on goods, services, property, or facilities that place a burden on the environment and include Mie prefecture's industrial waste landfill tax, the Tokyo city of Suginami's tax on plastic bags handed out by shops, and the water-source-conservation taxes under consideration in various locations.

The second category of taxes is aimed at promoting regional development, conservation, and disaster prevention. Such taxes, targeted mainly at tourists and residents from other areas, include the Shizuoka prefecture city of Atami's tax on vacation homes, the fishing taxes of municipalities bordering Lake Kawaguchi, in Yamanashi prefecture, Tokyo's hotel tax, and the mountain climbers' and hikers' taxes that various municipalities are considering.

The third category comprises taxes on corporations aimed at rectifying the instability of local tax bases that result from the heavy dependence of prefectures on the corporate enterprise tax, receipts from which fluctuate in response to economic conditions. One prominent example is Tokyo's so-called bank tax, which applies to the gross profits of major banks operating in the metropolis; there is also the temporary special corporate tax introduced by Kanagawa prefecture, according to which corporations are subject to taxation at a reduced rate on losses carried over from one business year to the next.

One of the effects resulting from the moves by local governments to introduce new taxes is the emergence of a degree of coordination among the tax and various other sections within local government bodies in considering tax affairs. Previously, when local governments had very little discretionary authority over their own tax systems, the linkage between taxation and policymaking was extremely tenuous. But now that the option of creating earmarked taxes has become available, local governments have room to consider taxation based on expected demand for revenues.

Another effect of the move by local governments to introduce new taxes is that coordination among them is becoming an important issue, since it is now technically possible for them to poach each other's revenue sources. For example, municipalities in major urban areas are likely to consider taxing emissions of industrial wastes, while municipalities in rural regions where the wastes are disposed of may well consider imposing disposal and landfill taxes. This is liable to mean taxation of wastes both at the source and at the location of final disposal which, because it may violate the requirement for consent from the central government, means that some degree of coordination may be needed to resolve the issue.

## THE DIRECTION OF REFORM

### Local Competition for Tax Revenues

If local governments are to administer their affairs autonomously, they must be able to secure sufficient revenues to cover the costs of their expanding roles. Inasmuch as the ability of the Local Allocation Tax to guarantee the necessary revenues has reached its limit, it is necessary to change the system by transferring tax sources (such as a portion of the national income tax, or a larger share of the consumption tax), to the regions so that local governments will be able to independently consider the supply of services and the handling of the resulting burdens.

While local governments have taken steps toward administrative and fiscal reform and toward a more decentralized society, a new problem has surfaced. Conflicts between central and local government, and among local governments, have emerged. Anticipating tax reform, each is seeking ways to increase their respective tax revenues. Generally, when grants are reduced and local taxes are expanded, the areas that benefit are few and specific; Tokyo is an example. While local governments may find such negotiations with the central government difficult, the scramble for tax revenues is not diminished. Further, local governments in a weaker financial position usually fear that local tax reform will reduce their central government grants and subsidies. Such local authorities may wish to change the restriction placed on their authority over grants-in-aid but, needing the subsidies, they do not wish to rock the boat. Meanwhile, a big city that has a sufficient source of taxation may want to collect its own revenues and so remove the tax resource from the national to the local level.[8]

The movement for new taxes in many regions has had the effect of creating unexpected competition among governments. Thus, for example, Tokyo and Osaka have opted for imposition of a corporate enterprise tax system—based on such considerations as sales and salaries—on banking institutions, which will have the effect of decreasing revenues from the corporate tax at the national level and the enterprise tax at the prefectural level.[9]

## Efforts to Cut Costs of Local Services

In order to create a self-sustaining, local fiscal system, current intergovernmental fiscal relations must be reconsidered, and reforming the system for greater local autonomy is warranted. But it is also important that, through reform, local governments be made aware of their own responsibilities and work to achieve greater effectiveness. Moreover, local governments must allow citizen participation in their administrations.

Amidst the crisis in local government finances, there is little that local governments can do to increase their tax revenues given the present system, so the most practical way for them to deal with the crisis is to cut spending. One trend that is evident nationwide is that of holding down personnel costs. The share of such costs as a percentage of local government spending has decreased gradually since the mid-1980s, and since the mid-1990s has been held at a level of around 25 percent. Given that the rising demand for interpersonal services would ordinarily mean higher personnel expenses, the fact that spending in this category has been kept basically flat suggests that local authorities have been making efforts to hold the line by various means including staff reductions.

Besides staff cutbacks, efforts to cut costs fall into three main areas. First are reforms within local government organs based on policy and operational evaluations. This approach seeks not only to review whether activities are necessary, but also to select effective means of supplying administrative services by considering possible alternatives to existing methods.

Second are moves to privatize government operations or to tap private-sector energy in providing public services. These include use of private finance initiative (PFI) in constructing and operating facilities, and entrusting the management of existing operations to private-sector bodies.

Third are the moves to cut costs through citizens participation, examples of which include the cooperation of neighborhood associations, local volunteer groups, and nonprofit organizations to provide interpersonal services through mutual aid at the grass-roots level. These efforts have been accompanied in some cases by moves to solidify the system of mutual aid through the introduction of a "community currency" as part of a local set of barter arrangements.

## The Government-Citizen Relationship

Fiscal transfers from the central government account for a great portion of the local government revenues, and this tends to cloud the relationship between benefits and burdens with respect to government services. If revenue sources were shifted to local governments, the benefit-burden relationships would become more clear, and taxpayer perceptions would be likely to change. Local government needs to institute and enforce rules on accountability, and devise local fiscal systems that match the needs of society. Since citizen participation in the decision-making process is important, government should facilitate the dissemination of information by sponsoring forums for discussion or offering venues where they might take place. As part of the administrative reforms, the movement for information disclosure and citizen participation in municipal affairs has spread rapidly across the country. Many local governments have responded by being more open about their financial situation, some going so far as to prepare balance sheets, or revealing the cost per capita of city hall, or cost-benefit analyses for public examination. Citizens are thereby gaining a better understanding of not only the financial situation in their region, but also of the cost of the public services they receive.

Recently, many local government bodies have been making active use of the Internet on an interactive basis, and using websites to convey information and gather input from the public on government services. Since 1995, the Kanagawa prefecture city of Yamato used the Internet to encourage citizen participation in the drafting of a master urban plan that was finalized in 1997, as a result of which the municipal government revamped its internal decision-making system so as to be able to respond promptly to the opinions and queries of residents. An increasing number of local governments are also using their websites to conduct bidding for public works projects. The city of Kamakura, Kanagawa prefecture, has taken this a step further, disclosing not just the winning bid, but the names of the bidders and the amounts of their bids.[10] Such an arrangement serves as a powerful deterrent to bid rigging.

Meanwhile, an increasing number of local governments are producing balance sheets and disclosing other fiscal information in an effort to present their financial situation in a form that is easily understood. Tokyo's Arakawa city has set up a website devoted to promoting residents' understanding of the city's finances, based on a policy of disclosing information and using indicators that will be clear to the general public.[11] The city uses it to disclose all the costs of operating its facilities, together with information on aspects of its finances, how the current critical economic situation is affecting it, and what countermeasures are planned; the emphasis is on presenting this information in a way that ward residents can readily grasp.

One other issue that local governments should address is rules of engagement for the supply of personal services in a municipality. For example, while nursing services can be supplied by various entities —the family, the municipality, private enterprise, and nonprofit organizations—it is important to study the situation locally, review the suppliers of services, and factor in the burden of expense. Some areas have already started to build nursing service systems using LETS (a local community exchange system) or time-saving systems. In these cases, the central government, regional groups, local companies, and communities have cooperated to build their own systems to supply local needs.

## FUTURE PROSPECTS

As we have seen in this chapter, local government finances are in a critical state and the central government's ability to guarantee the required revenues has reached its limit. Moreover, the central government has used local governments as tools in its efforts to stimulate the economy through public works projects, thereby having caused their tax revenues to decrease as a result of its antirecessionary tax cuts, and leaving them to bear heavy debt burdens. The current reform drive aims to impose responsibility on local governments without giving them local decision-making authority, while at the same time cutting their subsidies and Local Allocation Tax payments, thereby particularly aggravating the problems of those local governments already financially weak.

If our goal is to create a decentralized society in which the economic actors within each region will both make their own decisions about the quantity and quality of the public services they want to receive, and bear the corresponding burden, then we must create a system of local government finance in which the relationship between benefits and burdens is readily apparent. In this context, the division of revenue sources between the central government and local governments should, in principle, correspond to the division of operational authority. It is unreasonable to expect local governments to assume responsibility for their own affairs under the present setup, which requires them to carry out the bulk of the operations but allows them only weak tax bases.

There are also a host of issues that need to be addressed at the local level. Local governments will have to create systems of high transparency in the conduct of their administrative and financial affairs so as to gain the understanding of their citizens regarding proposed revenue-raising measures. In recognition of their accountability to taxpayers, local authorities must slash inefficient expenditures.

In a decentralized society, local governments have authority over their affairs and, within their respective jurisdictions, must form a positive relationship with their citizenry. To overcome the financial crisis, it is critical that there be a decision-making system involving all players in the local economy, so that the needs in terms of public services and the accompanying fiscal burden may be determined. It is only through the local decision-making system that financial decentralization can be viable, and the decentralization of government achieved.

## NOTES

1. Local government in Japan has two administrative levels: 47 prefectures and their division into about 3,200 municipalities, towns, and villages.

2. Looking at revenues from the two corporate taxes, we find that during the bubble economy, the total increased by close to 20 percent year on year, but in fiscal 1992–1993, following the bursting of the bubble, the figure dropped 15 percent year on year. The enterprise tax is highly susceptible to changes in

economic conditions, making it difficult for local governments to forecast their tax revenues.

3. About the relations between the trend of public works and Japan's foreign diplomacy policy, see Kanazawa (2002, chapter 1).

4. Interviews at the local affairs section of the Nagano Prefecture Government Office in December 1990.

5. Borrowing through the special account of the Local Allocation Tax has been criticized for its lack of transparency and the fact that ultimate responsibility for the loans is not clearly defined. See Miyajima (1987, chapters 3 and 7).

6. Researchers have determined that the actual amounts paid under the Local Allocation Tax system correspond basically to amounts that can be theoretically derived from just two factors, population and area, and this has served as the basis for strong arguments in favor of simplification of the calculation method.

7. Calculated using data from Ministry of Public Management, Home Affairs, Posts and Telecommunications (2000a).

8. A number of governments, including those of Tokyo, Kanagawa prefecture, and Osaka, have set up their own research groups to study what sort of reform would be most desirable for them and have conducted simulations of the possible effects of revenue source transfers. The government bodies have felt compelled to do so as decentralization has progressed and the crisis in government finances has worsened.

9. There are also differences in the apportionment of enterprise taxes collected from corporations that have business establishments in multiple tax jurisdictions.

10. URL <http://www.city.kamakura.kanagawa.jp/keiyaku/index.htm> (in Japanese).

11. URL <http://www.city.arakawa.tokyo.jp/hakusho2000/index_haku sho2000.html> (in Japanese).

## BIBLIOGRAPHY

Committeee for the Promotion of Decentralization. 2001. "Saishū hōkoku" (The final report). <http:www8.cao.go.jp/bunken/bunken-iinkai/saisyu> (8 July 2002).

Council of Economic and Fiscal Policy. 2001. "Kongo no keizai zaisei un'ei oyobi keizai shakai no kōzō kaikaku ni kansuru kihon hōshin" (Outline of basic policies for macroeconomic management and the structural reform of the Japanese economies). <http://www5.cao.go.jp/shimon/2001/0621outline-e.html>.

DeWit, Andrew. 2000. "Nihon no seifu-kan zaisei kankei no seijigakuteki bunseki" (Political science analysis on financial relations among local governments in Japan). Speech made at the 8th Japan Association of Local Public Finance Conference. 27 May.

Horie Fukashi and Nishio Masaru, eds. 1997. *Future Challenges of Local Autonomy in Japan, Korea, and the United States.* Tokyo: National Institute for Research Advancement.

Jinno Naohiko and Kaneko Masaru. 1998. *Chihō ni zeigen wo* (Transfer the national tax source to local regions). Tokyo: Tōyō-keizai Shimpō-sha.

Kanazawa Fumio, ed. 2002. *Gendai no kōkyō jigyō* (Public works in Japan and other countries). Tokyo: Nihon Keizai Hyōron-sha.

Ministry of Public Management, Home Affairs, Posts and Telecommunications. 2000a. "Chihō kōhuzei kankei keisū shiryō (Statistics of factors related to the Local Allocation Tax). Tokyo: Ministry of Public Management, Home Affairs, Posts and Telecommunications.

———. 2000b. *Data on Local Finance.* Tokyo: Ministry of Public Management, Home Affairs, Posts and Telecommunications.

———. 2001a. *Kazei jishuken no katsuyō ni mukete* (Local autonomy of taxation and its practical use). Tokyo: Jichi Sōgō Center.

———. 2001b. *White Paper on Local Finance.* Tokyo: Printing Division of Ministry of Finance.

Miyajima Hiroshi. 1987. *Zaisei saiken no kenkyū* (Fiscal reform in Japan). Tokyo: Yūhikaku.

Takeda Hiroshi. 1995. *Kōreisha fukushi no zaisei kadai* (Fiscal problems of social service for the elderly). Tokyo: Akebi Shobō.

The Government Tax Commission. 2000. "*Waga kuni zeisei no genjō to kadai* (The current situation and issues regarding the Japanese taxation system—working for participation and making choices towards the 21st century). <http://www.mof.go.jp/english/tosin/tax/tax001.htm>.

# 7

# The Emergence of NPOs and the Implications for Local Governance

## Tamura Shigeru

In Japan, the public sector has been the main actor in governance for many decades, and at the local level in particular, local governments have been dominant in providing public services. Although there are some private entities such as electricity suppliers and neighborhood associations that provide public services, they are supervised and supported by the public sector because it is responsible for the quality and quantity of public services. There has, thus, been a strong tendency for the Japanese people to overly rely on the government when faced with problems.

However, as social circumstances have changed due to the rapid aging of the population, worsening environmental problems, the expansion of internationalization, the diversification of citizen demands, and the Great Hanshin-Awaji Earthquake in 1995, the number of people serving as volunteers has increased and nonprofit organizations (NPOs) have come to play an increasingly significant role in local governance. This chapter looks at the development and major characteristics of NPOs in Japan, their relationship with local governments in an era of decentralization, and how conflicts between NPOs and government might be resolved. To this end, consideration is given to the questions of how local governments can support NPOs, the areas for which local governments should take responsibility, and how NPOs can be held accountable in their partnerships with local governments.

## THE DEVELOPMENT OF NPOS

### Government Corruption and the Need for Reform

After the Meiji Restoration (1868), in its bid to catch up with the economic advances of Western countries, Japan introduced a centralized administrative system, which framework remained after World War II. While by 1970 Japan had attained a position in the top echelon of international economic development largely due to its administrative system, once the bubble had burst in the 1990s, it was precisely this system that came under severe criticism. No longer did the citizens regard the bureaucracy as completely trustworthy, and a pall fell over the government due to corruption and the mismanagement of public policy, especially in the area of finance.

The belief that increased investment in public works would stimulate the economy, despite decreasing tax revenues, led the central and local governments to borrow funds, and the public debt came to exceed the nation's gross domestic product (GDP). This forced the government to recognize the need for administrative reform: a reassessment of the role of the public sector, a drastic power shift from the public to the private sector, and deregulation.

As a part of administrative reform, decentralization must be encouraged. For while in the 1940s and 1950s local governments certainly lacked the human and financial resources to shoulder greater responsibility, this is no longer the case. Since the enforcement of the 1995 Law for Promoting Decentralization and the 1999 Omnibus Law of Decentralization, the relationship between the central and local governments has been gradually changing.

### Changes in Local Governance

According to a national survey conducted by the Ministry of Health, Labour and Welfare in 2000, over one-sixth of Japan's population was aged 65 or over, while in some rural municipalities those in that age bracket represented more than 40 percent of the population.[1] This is due partly to increased life expectancy and partly to the decreased birth rate. The fast graying of society caused the central government to reform the pension scheme and introduce a special healthcare insurance system for the aged in 2000. Since welfare services for the aged are provided by municipalities and social welfare foundations, the growing number of elderly has meant that local and particularly municipal governments face an increasing social welfare burden. Pressure is already building to shift the emphasis from the uniform services provided to date by local governments, to more customized services, as are already being provided by some NPOs.

With regard to environmental problems, local government policies have always been ahead of those of the central government. In the 1960s and 1970s, local governments' successive antipollution measures lead to enactment of the Basic Law for Environmental Pollution Control in 1967 and the setting up, in 1971, of the then Environment Agency (now called the Ministry of the Environment). With the recent and evolving concern about global environmental issues and the promotion of recycling, the cooperation of the populace—both victims and polluters—is vital, and it is in this regard that NPOs have been performing energetically in many places.

The provision of social services is also inextricably linked to Japan's policy concerning foreign residents, whose numbers have doubled over the past 25 years. While the central government controls immigration, it is up to local governments to see that foreign residents receive social services. Since local governments often find themselves strapped for resources, NPOs have often stepped into the breach to provide the requisite services for these residents. Matters concerning undocumented migrants pose a raft of completely different problems, and these individuals often receive support from NPOs rather than local government authorities.

## Diversification of Citizens' Demands

With economic growth, work-related stress levels have risen and so, in turn, people's expectations and social demands have diversified. According to a 1999 survey conducted by the then Prime Minister's

Office, the number of respondents who indicated that they value mental rather than material enrichment had risen to 57.0 percent from 36.7 percent in 1974, while the number of those who indicated that they value leisure and hobbies rather than their occupations had risen to 32.3 percent from 13.8 percent in 1974. Many people seem to have come to believe that one's job is not the most important thing in life, which has led to an increase in the number of individuals electing to serve as volunteers or participate in NPOs.

At the same time, people's expectations of NPOs are changing, as they recognize that these groups are well placed to manage the time constraints of volunteers so as to provide continuous service, as well as sources of accumulated expertise and special skills. As government corruption has caused many to distrust the public sector and changing social conditions have influenced local governance, many people have come to see volunteer work and NPOs as avenues to help resolve regional problems.

## The Place of NPOs in Japan

In Japan, NPOs are variously defined. In some surveys neighborhood associations are included and in others not. According to the Economic Planning Agency, there are four categories (fig. 1) of NPOs (Economic Planning Agency 2000b, 130): specified nonprofit corporations (none existed until 1998; referred to in the agency's white paper), which comprise the narrowest definition of the term; volunteer and civic groups (also referred to in the agency's white paper); corporate juridical persons, foundations, and social welfare, school, religious, and medical corporations that include some for-profit organizations; and labor unions as well as economic and cooperative associations. The agency acknowledges that neighborhood associations, which are location-specific, are sometimes included as a category of NPO.

According to the Economic Planning Agency's 1996 survey of civic groups[2]—Japan's first survey of NPOs—there were 85,786 such organizations (Economic Planning Agency 1997, 1–14), of which 37 percent were engaged mainly in social services; 17 percent in community activities; 17 percent in education, culture, and sports activities; 10 percent in environmental conservation; 5 percent in healthcare- and medical care-related services; and 5 percent in international exchanges.

Figure 1. Organizations Defined as Nonprofit Organizations*

| | | | |
|---|---|---|---|
| | 1 | Specified nonprofit corporations | The narrowest definition |
| | 2 | Volunteer groups | As defined by the Economic Planning Agency white paper |
| | | Civic groups | |
| Organizations for Public Profit | 3 | Corporate juridical persons | |
| | | Foundations | As generally defined in the United States |
| | | Social welfare corporations | |
| | | School corporations | The broadest definition |
| | | Religious corporations | |
| | | Medical corporations | |
| | | Neighborhood associations | |
| Organizations for Common Profit | 4 | Labor Union | |
| | | Economic Association | |
| | | Cooperative Association | |

*Source:* Economic Planning Agency (2000b).

*Neighborhood associations are included as nonprofit organizations as an exception.

The survey also shows that the history of NPOs in Japan is short, 26 percent having started their activities before 1976, 44 percent after 1985, and 24 percent between 1976 and 1985. In addition, about two-thirds had a membership system, of which 44 percent had fewer than 50 members, while one-third of NPOs had annual expenses of less than ¥100,000[3] and, on average, one-third of their revenue was derived from membership fees, one-third from subsidies, and 13 percent from business, with donations accounting for only 5 percent. It was also revealed that 69 percent of NPOs had administrative staff, of which 82 percent had part-time staff, 31 percent full-time staff, and 23 percent paid staff. Of the staff, 40 percent were homemakers, 28 percent civil servants or public entity employees, and 25 percent retirees. From these figures it can be seen that Japanese NPOs are relatively vulnerable to the effects of financial and structural change.

This survey also investigated the demands of NPOs, and reveals that more than 80 percent required government support, over 75 percent public-sector financial aid, some 49 percent free use of office space, 48 percent facilities and equipment, and 45 percent relevant training.

According to a 1997 Economic Planning Agency survey (Economic Planning Agency 1998, 5–26), the total economic value of services provided by all types of NPOs in 1995 was ¥15 trillion, or 3.1 percent of GDP.[4] In 1998, the figure had risen to ¥18 trillion, or 3.6 percent of GDP (Economic Planning Agency 2000b, 131). Medical care constituted the largest share (46 percent) of NPO outlays, followed by education (28 percent), and social services (13 percent). Most of the organizations included in these three types of NPO represent the older groups, which comprise hospitals, social welfare organizations, and private schools; their outlays were somewhat higher than those of newer NPOs—civic groups—the outlays of which totaled a modest ¥30 billion in 1998.

## The Rise of Corporate NPOs

Until the enactment of the December 1998 Law to Promote Specified Nonprofit Activities, or NPO Law, there had been only two ways to incorporate organizations, namely, by applying the Civil Code (to create corporate juridical persons and foundations), or by applying such individual laws as the Private School Law (to create school corporations) or the Social Welfare Law (to create social welfare corporations). While being incorporated makes it easier for organizations to gain social trust or raise funds, the legal procedure under these laws is complex and the legal treatment of nonprofit organizations in Japan is highly restrictive and rigid (Amemiya 1998, 59). Consequently, small organizations often remained unincorporated despite inconveniences such as having to sign legal documents or open bank accounts using the name of an individual member rather than the name of the organization.

The NPO Law aimed to contribute to the public interest by promoting the sound development of nonprofit activities, which it divided into 12 groups (Cabinet Office 2001b):
- Health, social welfare
- Social education
- Community development
- Culture, arts, and sports

- Environmental protection
- Disaster-relief activities
- Community safety
- Human rights and international peace
- International cooperation
- The creation of a gender-equal society
- The sound nurturing of youth
- Liaising, advising, and support activities related to organizations performing any of the aforementioned activities.

According to this law, the term NPO refers to an organization that is incorporated in accordance with the provisions of this law (Cabinet Office 2001b) and can further be defined as one that:

1) Does not seek to make a profit, while neither
   a) attaching unreasonable importance to gaining or losing membership status, nor
   b) having more than one-third of its officers receive remuneration.
2) Does not have as its main purpose
   a) the spreading of religious doctrine, performing of religious services or rituals, or preaching;
   b) the promotion, support, or opposition of political principles; or
   c) the recommendation, support, or opposition of a candidate for a certain public office (or a person who aims to be a candidate for said office), a public official, or a political party.

In addition, the NPO Law requires that NPOs should have ten or more members, and may engage in profit-making projects provided that the profits are used for nonprofit activities and do not interfere with nonprofit activities. Further, it stipulates that prefectural governors shall serve as the competent authorities (those who grant incorporated status) for those NPOs that establish an office or offices in prefectures, and the national government shall commission the prefectures to perform the relevant duties concerning granting incorporated status. In the event that NPOs set up offices in two or more prefectures, it is required by law that the Cabinet Office (then Minister of the Economic Planning Agency) shall serve as their competent authority. It is also required by the NPO Law that the legal requirements concerning NPOs shall be reviewed within three years of the day the law went into effect, and that the measures deemed necessary shall be formulated on the basis of the results of the review.

Some 67 percent of Japan's incorporated NPOs operate in the field of healthcare and social welfare, 33 percent in community development, 32 percent in the nurturing of youth, and 30 percent in social education (Economic Planning Agency 2000a, 21).[5] As of March 2001, the number of incorporated NPOs had risen to 3,295 (Cabinet Office 2001a, 1–2), about 40 percent of which are located in densely populated areas such as Tokyo (818), Osaka (244), and Kanagawa prefecture (236), while about two-thirds of those NPOs with offices in two or more prefectures have their main offices in Tokyo, indicating that NPOs are more active in urban than rural areas.

According to a 1999 Economic Planning Agency (2000a, 4–5) survey, three-quarters of the incorporated NPOs had already been involved in their present activities before incorporation, although half were established after the Great Hanshin-Awaji Earthquake in 1995. Of the total, about 40 percent had fewer than 50 members, 37 percent had annual revenues of more than ¥10 million, and two-fifths had no donation revenue. Meanwhile, 68 percent had full-time staff, but only 2 percent had 10 or more members or staff. About 60 percent had some links with the public sector, from which 25 percent received subsidies, 20 percent trustees, and 18 percent office space. The surveys indicate that, in general, while incorporated NPOs were somewhat larger than their unincorporated counterparts, there was otherwise little difference between the two categories.

Besides the surveys conducted by the government, there are also some carried out by NPOs. According to a 2000 survey of incorporated NPOs conducted by an individual NPO (C's 2000a, 1–5), about 60 percent were dissatisfied with the NPO Law, mainly because it lacks tax incentives: Donations to NPOs cannot be deducted for taxation purposes. Since donations help support NPO activities, a review of the NPO Law requires that donations are to be tax deductible commencing in October 2001.

The NPO-conducted survey also reveals that about half the NPOs surveyed recognized that competition exists between the government and NPOs, two-thirds of the NPOs believing that they can provide services better suited to user needs, 46 percent that they can provide more flexible service, and 43 percent that their services have greater citizen appeal. In contrast, 44 percent of the polled NPOs admitted that their services were not recognized as being sufficiently reliable, more than three-fourths stressed the need for evaluation by those on the receiving end of their services, 57 percent stressed the need for evaluation by supporters or NPO members, and less than 40 percent stressed the need for evaluation by outsiders or specialists.

## JAPANESE AND U.S. NPOS, VOLUNTEERING COMPARED

The 2000 white paper put out by the Economic Planning Agency on the national lifestyle is the first to address the subject of volunteering, and compares some of the relevant activities conducted in Japan and other countries, especially the United States.

The number of volunteers is increasing steadily and, by 1996 one out of four Japanese had done volunteer work. However, the figure is less than half that for the United States across all age brackets, and is particularly low for the younger generation. There are many differences between the two countries in terms of incentives and reasons for which people become involved in volunteer work (Economic Planning Agency 2000b, 54–55). According to the white paper (table 1), 72.7 percent of Japanese and 68.0 percent of U.S. nationals indicated in surveys that they had become involved in volunteering to "insure the continuation of activities or institutions I or my family benefit from"; the phrase "feel that those who have more should help those with less" was chosen as most appropriate by 63.2 percent of the Japanese and 83.7 percent of the U.S. respondents; "gain a sense of personal

Table 1. Motivation for Giving and Volunteering in Japan and the United States

| Motivating Factors | Japan (%) | United States (%) |
|---|---|---|
| Insuring the continuation of activities or institutions me or my family benefit from | 72.7 | 68.0 |
| Feeling that those who have more should help those with less | 63.2 | 83.7 |
| Fulfilling a business or community obligation | 53.1 | 58.5 |
| Gaining a sense of personal satisfaction | 50.4 | 81.6 |
| Giving back to society some of the benefits it gave you | 48.1 | 74.4 |
| Being asked to contribute or volunteer by a personal friend of business associate | 46.4 | 70.8 |
| Donating as a personal legacy or in memory of a family member | 37.2 | 50.8 |
| Being encouraged by an employer | 34.1 | 43.3 |
| Serving as an example to others | 33.9 | 68.8 |

*Source:* Economic Planning Agency (2000b).

satisfaction" by 50.4 percent of the Japanese and 81.6 percent of the U.S. respondents; "as a personal legacy or in memory of a family member" by 37.2 percent of Japanese and 50.8 percent of U.S. respondents; and "serving as an example to others" by 33.9 percent of Japanese and 68.8 percent of U.S. respondents.

In terms of donations per household, the funds given annually in the United States (the equivalent of ¥98,000) in 1998 were more than 30 times as large as donations in Japan (¥3,200) in 1999. In the United States, besides the donations that accounted for only 13 percent of NPOs' total resources, membership fees and charges for services accounted for 57 percent, and public-sector subsidies 30 percent. In Japan, donations accounted for 3 percent, membership fees and charges for services 52 percent, and public-sector subsidies 45 percent (Economic Planning Agency 2000b, 157).

From these results, it can be seen that the activities of acquaintances and a sense of obligation have often caused people to volunteer in Japan, whereas a desire for personal satisfaction was a relatively strong motivator in the United States, and few in Japan considered "serving as an example to others" as a reason to volunteer.

Based on the survey results mentioned above, NPOs in Japan can be described as follows: In 1998, 3.6 percent of GDP was derived from the country's 85,000 NPOs (the number as of 1996 and excluding corporate juridical persons and foundations), most of which were small and financially poor, and more than 80 percent of which thought they should receive public-sector support. Some 3,000 organizations had been newly incorporated by 1998. A 2000 survey of 1,034 incorporated NPOs revealed that about 60 percent were dissatisfied with the NPO Law.

## LOCAL GOVERNMENT–NPO RELATIONS

### Bilateral Cooperation

The fact that more than two-thirds of the public-sector expenditure is spent by local governments underlines the importance of this level of public administration. However, until enforcement of the Omnibus Law of Decentralization in April 2000, the central government controlled local affairs through the agency-delegated function (ADF) system, which had the effect of diluting responsibility in government and eroding local autonomy. Even before the Decentralization Law, the central government had shifted its emphasis to the promotion of decentralization, recognizing that local affairs should be decided according to local conditions, and now expects local governments and NPOs to play key roles in local governance. In this context, three types of NPOs can be identified, namely, those that have no connection with local government, those that seek to foster good relations with local government, and those that, while not connected, keep a weather eye on local government activities (Shimin Katsudō 2000, 15–21).

Those NPOs that are trying to build good relations with local governments are taking four approaches. First, some seek to provide directly those public services entrusted to them by local government authorities; second, much as do neighborhood associations, they support and provide community activities; third, they encourage citizen participation in local governance; and fourth, they play a coordinating role in those projects that involve local government, private-sector companies, and local citizens.

## Local Government Support

Since the 1990s, NPOs have been performing an ever-broader variety of activities. When local governments delegate functions and services to NPOs, they expect that the services provided will match more closely the needs of citizens than have previous government efforts, and even that new services will be provided which authorities have previously been unable to provide. However, since NPOs generally find themselves in financial straits, some are receiving local government support for their enterprises.

As of July 2000, 11 local governments have enacted bylaws enabling them to promote and support local NPOs (C's 2000b). While some of these bylaws deal only with the abstract, others (as is the case with the Tohoku area capital, Sendai city) mention setting up support centers, or (Osaka's Minoo city) state that, should the city outsource functions, NPOs should be considered possible contractors. The central Japan prefecture of Mie, however, has taken a different tack. Well known for its progressive style of administration, after much deliberation the prefecture decided against enacting an NPO-related bylaw, in the belief that if NPOs are to be independent and voluntary enterprises, such a bylaw might be interpreted as interference. Instead, a declaration of partnership was issued.

As of July 2000, there were some 47 NPO support centers, 16 of which were managed by local governments, and 31 by NPOs themselves (C's 2000c, 1–5). These centers allow NPOs to use their facilities as office space and for meetings at no or very little cost. They provide NPOs with useful information, conduct training courses for prospective volunteers and NPO staff, provide management advice, and increasingly give monetary support, thereby allowing NPOs to gradually play an increasingly significant role in local governance.

## BILATERAL PARTNERSHIPS

In local governance, a crucial issue for local government has become partnership: not only with people and private-sector companies, but also with NPOs, in connection with which they need to step away from the support phase. Mie prefecture, for example, is second only to Tokyo in terms of the large number of NPOs per capita. Mie is the first local government to evaluate public administration, and more recently introduced a system, in cooperation with NPOs, whereby its administration would be assessed from the point of view of service recipients (Kogawa 1999, 19–31). Four measures are used: budget and planning, implementation, citizen-participation and openness, and contribution to civil society. To insure the optimum functioning of the new system—which considers people to be service recipients, providers, and evaluators—a new NPO, Evaluation Mie, was established to assess the prefecture's work from the citizens' stance, and NPOs are encouraged to participate in planning prefectural policy.

## BILATERAL COMPETITION

As local governments have increased their support for NPOs, their activities have certainly been revitalized but, on occasion, government activities have been in direct competition, or interfered, with NPO activities.

A case in point is that of a social welfare service begun in 1996 in Osaka city. Accordingly, city sanitation workers collected the garbage bags of the elderly and infirm that had been left at their doors, rather than at local garbage collection points which they could not easily reach. This new service has been well received, especially by those living in high-rise housing.

The Osaka city workers union introduced the service in a bid to avert employee cutbacks, but found itself at loggerheads with NPOs, which claimed that they could also provide this kind of social service, and voiced concern that garbage collectors might even in the future see fit to provide other welfare services as if they were trained social caseworkers. Had Osaka first discussed which services local government should provide and which should be outsourced and to which organizations, acrimony could have been avoided and the service might not have been provided by the city's sanitation workers.

The NPO support centers established and managed by local governments are often examples of interference with NPO activities. Such publicly organized centers might be necessary in rural areas, where NPOs are not so active, but in urban areas where their activities are vital, local governments should avoid setting up new support centers, reconsider the role of the existing centers, and entrust their management to NPOs. Local governments should avoid interfering with the development of NPOs and, where support is given, set the terms and conditions, especially where monetary support is involved, to ensure that NPOs do not become dependent on the public sector.

## NATIONAL GOVERNMENT–NPO RELATIONS

### Bilateral Competition

It is not unknown for the central government to be perceived as obstructing the development of NPOs. In 1994, for example, the then-Ministry of Labor (which became the Ministry of Health, Labour and Welfare in 2000) established the Family Support Center Program to help parents who, for work-related reasons or other considerations, wish to have their children looked after at times when nurseries and schools are closed. The program mainly targets working women who find it hard to juggle work commitments and household chores. Municipalities are encouraged to set up family support centers where those who want to leave their children (requesting members) and those who want to look after them (supporting members) can register. A problem arose, however, when the ministry would provide only local governments with subsidies to support the management of these centers (Jiji Tsūshin-sha 2000, 8–9), even though some NPOs are also managing similar centers.

Another instance of perceived NPO obstruction concerns a 2000 plan by the then-Ministry of Education, Science, Sports and Culture (in 2001 reorganized as the Ministry of Education, Culture, Sports, Science and Technology) to mandate each municipality to establish a regional sports club within ten years from 2001 to promote sports and increase the number of Japanese medallists in the Olympic Games (Mombushō Hoken Taiiku Shingikai 2000). One of the ministry's targets was to increase the number of adults who participate in sports at least once a week from 35 percent to 50 percent. Most sports activities had previously been supported by schools and private companies, but the ministry wished to encourage a more European approach, according to which citizens would be encouraged to join regional sports clubs, which the ministry recommended should have the status of corporations under the NPO Law.

This example is not unlike other cases in which foundations have been established by local governments at the behest of the central government, which regards them as quasi-governmental organizations (quangos) or a means of achieving a national blueprint. Not only do many citizens believe that it should not be necessary for every local government to establish a sports club, but also that the central government should allow local governments and residents to decide how such sports clubs are managed once local consent has been achieved concerning their establishment.

### An NPO Perspective

Many NPOs have been insisting that they be granted a tax-exempt status similar to that found in the United States. Although donations to NPOs were made tax deductible in October 2001, NPOs continue to complain: first, of the strict conditions that are to govern such gifts and, second, that the activities of NPOs are not tax exempt. It is possible that, were the two complaints resolved, the financial situation of NPOs would improve; but as the U.S. case has shown, it is almost impossible to successfully manage NPOs relying only on donations, so the public sector will inevitably be called on, for some time yet, to supply some portion of the necessary resources.

Recently, transparency and accountability have become the buzz words applied by the public to all aspects of public administration, including the spending of taxes at the local level, and by local governments to evaluating public administration. NPOs, which have come to shoulder some responsibility for local governance, should bear this trend in mind when seeking to command the confidence and support of citizens.

Inevitably, there are those local government officials who view every NPO as opposing the public sector, and NPOs—particularly citizen ombudsmen—that observe and monitor the activities of local governments as a nuisance. But since these officials in many cases lack a proper understanding of NPOs, local governments would be wise to provide such officials with training in the intricacies of NPOs.

It should be borne in mind that citizen ombudsmen-type NPOs have emerged recently in response to the malfunctioning of local legislative assemblies, made up of directly elected councillors, that determine budgets, enact local legislation, and make political decisions. Had the functions of local assemblies been properly discharged, this kind of NPO might not have emerged. Through the system of public information disclosure implemented by many local governments, these NPOs have levied accusations concerning illegally spent public funds, particularly on unauthorized travel, and have helped compensate for the shortcomings of the existing system by pressuring offending parties to implement redress. Local governments might well be pleased.

Yet it could be argued that it would be better were NPOs not only to criticize local-government activities, but also to propose steps whereby public administration could be reformed and local think tanks strengthened. Constructive proposals would help change the attitude of local officials and lead citizens to recognize NPOs as important stakeholders in local governance. At the same time, NPOs must be seen to be accountable and reliable by both government officials and the general populace. In particular, NPO activities supported by local governments must be strictly evaluated, given that a portion of their resources is derived from the public sector. To this end, some NPOs have recently began seeking ways of using outside institutions to evaluate their activities.[6]

## CONCLUSION

NPOs face a number of difficulties, including a fragile revenue structure, problems associated with increasing membership and recruiting staff, and the worries associated with finding office and activity space. Thus, while respecting their independence, local governments need to support NPOs by, for example, extending administrative help, providing the information necessary to allow links to be forged between citizens and NPOs, and giving intermediary support with other organizations.

Certainly local governments have experience with financial adversity. Due to the country's economic woes, their tax income has not increased as expected, although they have had to spend a huge portion for their public investments to boost their regional economies. Many local governments have thus had to issue bonds, promote administrative reform and decentralization, and try to better coordinate the functioning of local stakeholders, including NPOs. In the area of administrative reform, local governments should restrict their role as public service providers to avoid duplicating the services of NPOs, especially in the fields of healthcare, welfare, social education, and community development. It is also important that the role of local government as a service provider be decided, not by local governments alone, but by thorough debate involving local stakeholders, including NPOs.

While the role of local governments might best be restricted to the areas of safety-related functions (the police and fire fighting) and regulation (environmental protection and food sanitation), local governments would be well advised to develop good relations with NPOs, regarding them as partners rather than as administrative subcontractors or local quangos, with a view to cooperating and sharing responsibilities with them.

It is said that the late eighteenth and the nineteenth centuries were the age of the night-watch state, and the twentieth century that of the welfare state. The twenty-first century might, therefore, be called the age of the citizen state, during which period NPOs assume greater responsibility for local governance, while gaining the understanding and appreciation of citizens who support them by becoming members and volunteering their time and skills. It is, indeed, citizens who foster NPOs, which must remember that accountability and transparency are the keys to good local governance.

## NOTES

1. The ratio of residents aged 65 and over is highest in the town of Tōwa, Yamaguchi prefecture, where as of October 1, 1999, this age group accounted for more than 50 percent of the population.

2. In 1996, specified nonprofit corporations did not yet exist.

3. In fiscal 1995, 35 percent of NPOs had annual expenses totaling less than ¥100,000, 43 percent less than ¥1 million, 18 percent less than ¥10 million, and only 4 percent ¥10 million or more.

4. Another survey gives a higher figure of 4.5 percent of GDP (Yamauchi, Shimizu, and Wojciech 1999, 244).

5. Multiple responses.

6. Two examples are Project Evaluation System for Nonprofit Organizations, set up in 1999 by the Sasakawa Peace Foundation, and the Research Committee for Evaluation System, set up in 2000 by the NPO Training and Resource Center, both of which organizations are studying how NPO activities might best be evaluated.

## BIBLIOGRAPHY

Amemiya Takao. 1998. "The Nonprofit Sector: Legal Background." In Yamamoto Tadashi, ed. *The Nonprofit Sector in Japan*. Manchester and New York: Manchester University Press.

Cabinet Office, ed. 2001a. *Tokutei hieiri katsudō sokushin hō ni motozuku shinsei juri sū oyobi ninshō sū funinshō sū zantei sū* (Applications and acceptances under the Law to Promote Specified Nonprofit Activities). <http://www.epa.go.jp/98/19981217c-npojyuri.html> (23 March).

———, ed. 2001b. *Outline of the Law to Promote Specified Nonprofit Activities*. <http://www5.cao.go.jp/98/c/19980319c-npo-e.html> (10 June).

C's (Coalition for Legistlation to Support Citizens' Organizations). 2000a. "'Enupīō hōjin no genjō to jigyō no arikata' shūkai hōkoku" (Report on the meeting to discuss NPO corporations. <http://c-s.vcom.or.jp/0802/report05.html> (11 September).

———. 2000b. "Jichitai jōhō" (Local government information). <http://c-s.vcom.or.jp/0502/0502(02).html> (11 September).

———. 2000c. "Enupīō shien sentā adoresu ichiran" (Addresses of NPO support centers). <http://www.jca.apc.org/jnpoc/support/sc_list.html> (13 November).

Economic Planning Agency, ed. 1997. *Shimin katsudō repōto* (Civil activities report). Tokyo: Ōkurashō Insatsu-kyoku.

———, ed. 1998. *Nihon no enupīō no keizai kibo* (Economic scale of Japanese NPOs). Tokyo: Ōkurashō Insatsu-kyoku.

———, ed. 2000a. *Tokutei hieiri katsudō hōjin no katsudō un'ei no jittai ni kansuru chōsa* (Investigating the activities and management of specified nonprofit corporations). Tokyo: Ōkurashō Insatsu-kyoku.

———, ed. 2000b. *Heisei jyūninendo kokumin seikatsu hakusho* (The white paper on the national lifestyle in fiscal year 2000). Tokyo: Ōkurashō Insatsu-kyoku.

Jiji Tsūshin-sha. 2000. *Kanchō sokuhō.* (Ministry-related news flash). Jiji Tsūshin-sha (20 October).

Kogawa Ichirō. 1999. "Shimin ni yoru jigyōhyōka shisutemu no koremade korekara" (Past and future of the citizens' project evaluation system). *Asu no Mie* 114:19–31.

Mombushō Hoken Taiiku Shingikai. 2000. "*Supōtsu shinkō kihon keikaku no arikata ni tsuite: yutaka na supōtsu kankyō wo mezashite* (The target of the sports activities promotion plan: A rich environment for sports). <http://www.monbu.go.jp/singi/hoken/00000255/> (19 September).

Shimin Katsudō to Gyōsei no Pātonāshippu no Arikata ni kansuru Kenkyūkai. 2000. "Shimin katsudō dantai to gyōsei no pātonāshippu no arikatani kansuru kenkyū-hōkoku" (Report on research concerning the improvement of the relationship between civic groups and public administration). Report presented to the Ministry of Home Affairs.

Yamauchi Naoto, Shimizu Hideko, and S. Wojciech. 1999. "Japan." In Lester M. Salamon et al., eds. *Global Civil Society: Dimensions of the Nonprofit Sector.* Baltimore, Md.: The Johns Hopkins Center for Civil Society Studies.

# About the Contributors

FURUKAWA SHUN'ICHI is Professor of Government and Public Administration, Institute of Policy and Planning Sciences, University of Tsukuba. Between 1971 and 1994, he worked at the Ministry of Home Affairs (now the Ministry of Public Management, Home Affairs, Posts and Telecommunications), where he held positions in the Bureau of Finance, as well as prefectural posts such as Director of the Office of Finance of Gifu prefecture and Director General of Economic Development of Nagasaki prefecture. Professor Furukawa is a graduate of the University of Tokyo's Department of Law. He studied public management and political science as a graduate student of Harvard University and obtained an M.A. in city and regional planning. He earned his Ph.D. in political science from the University of Tsukuba in 1998. During his 1986–1987 posting as Secretary-General of the Council of Local Authorities for International Relations (CLAIR), Professor Furukawa was involved in the establishment of the Japan Education and Teaching (JET) Programme. Until 1994, he was Director General of the Training Department of the Japan International Academy of Municipalities, responsible for overseeing programs designed to develop administrative capabilities of municipal personnel in relation to international needs of local regions. His major publications include *Kōkyō keiei to jōhō tsūshin gijutsu* (Public management and information and communication technologies, 2002),

*Kōkō bumon hyōka no riron to jissai* (Public sector evaluation in theory and practice, 2001), and *Renpōsei: Kyūkyoku no chihō bunken* (Federal system: Ultimate decentralization, 1993).

MENJU TOSHIHIRO is Senior Program Officer at the Japan Center for International Exchange (JCIE). After working for the Hyogo prefectural government he joined JCIE in 1988, where he is in charge of research on international activities by local governments as well as conducting exchange programs. He also serves as Research Fellow at the Tokyo Foundation. Mr. Menju is author of "A New Paradigm of North-South Relations" in *Cities and the Environment* (1999) and *Chikyū shimin nettowāku* (Network of global citizens, 1997), and co-author of several books, including *Ajia no NPO* (NPOs in Asia, 1997). He currently serves as a member of the Selection Committee for NGO Assistance Programs of the Ministry of Foreign Affairs and as a lecturer at Shizuoka University of Art and Culture. Mr. Menju is a graduate of Keio University and obtained an M.A. in public administration from Evergreen State College in Washington in 1986.

KANAGAWA KŌJI is Associate Professor of the Faculty of Social and Environmental Studies, Fukuoka Institute of Technology. He had been with the Hyōgo prefectural government for 21 years serving in the commerce and industry section and as a researcher with the prefecture's 21st Century Hyōgo Project Association. Professor Kanagawa was graduated from Waseda University and obtained an M.A. in policy science from Saitama University's Graduate School (currently the National Graduate Institute for Policy Studies) in 1986. He has contributed papers on local communities and NPOs to various publications, some of which are: "Kaigo hoken ka ni okeru enupīō no yakuwari to kadai" (Roles and problems of NPOs under the long-term care insurance) in *Seikatsu keizaigaku kenkyū* (Household economics research, 2002), and "Keikan hozen ni okeru kankō oyobi torasuto shuhō no igi to sono yakuwari" (The importance and role of tourism and the environment trust campaign for view preservation in *Borantarī keizai to komyuniti* (Voluntary economics and community, 2000)

KASHIWAZAKI CHIKAKO is Associate Professor of the Faculty of Economics at Keio University. She obtained a Ph.D. in sociology from

Brown University in 1998 and taught at Sophia University until moving to Keio University in 2001. Professor Kashiwazaki's major research areas are nationality and citizenship, ethnicity, and immigration policy. Her recent publications include "Politics of Legal Status: The Equation of Nationality with Ethnonational Identity" in *Koreans in Japan: Critical Voices from the Margin* (2000), "Citizenship in Japan: Legal Practice and Contemporary Development" in *From Migrants to Citizens* (2000), and "Kokuseki no arikata: Bunkateki tayōsei no shōnin ni mukete" (What nationality should be: Toward the recognition of cultural diversity) in *Gaikokujin no hōteki chii to jinken yōgo* (The legal status of foreign nationals and their human rights protection, 2002).

NAKAMURA MADOKA is Senior Researcher at the Center for Policy Research Information, National Institute for Research Advancement (NIRA). Graduated from Sophia University, she obtained an M.A. in sociology from the University of Tokyo's Institute for Socio-Information and Communication Studies, Graduate School of Humanities and Sociology. She was a visiting scholar at Cambridge University in the United Kingdom from 1996 to 1997 and a coordinator of *NIRA Review*, a quarterly English-language journal, from 1997 to 2001. Her recent publications include: *"Kōkyō seisaku jinzai yōsei puroguramu" sakutei ni kansuru kenkyū hōkoku* (Program design of the "syllabus for public policy research coordinators," co-authored, 2002), "Shinku tanku komyuniti no henkaku ni mukete" (Aims and objectives of think tanks and policy research) in *NIRA seisaku kenkyū* (NIRA policy research, 2001), and "Toward the Public Interest?: Transformation of the Policy Community in Japan" in *NIRA Review* (2000)

NUMAO NAMIKO is Associate Professor in the College of Economics at Nihon University. She was graduated from Keio University and earned an M.A. in economics from Keio University Graduate School of Economics in 1991. Before joining Nihon University, she served as Research Associate in the Faculty of Economics at Keio University from 1994 to 1997 and Research Fellow in the Tokyo Institute for Municipal Research from 1997 to 2000. She is the author of "Chihō zaisei seido kaikaku no hōkōsei: Jiritsu shita chihōken kakuritsu ni mukete" (The course of local finance system reform: Toward the establishment of independent local communities) in *Seikatsu keizai seisaku* (Household economic policy, 2002) and "Josei no katsuyaku wo hoshō suru zei shakai seido" (The tax and social security system securing women's social activities) in *ESP* (2001). She also co-authored "'Koizumi kaizō naikaku' e no taikō teian" (The counter proposal against "Koizumi structural reform") in *Sekai* (2001).

TAMURA SHIGERU is Associate Professor, Faculty of Law at Niigata University. After graduating from the University of Tokyo's Faculty of Engineering, Professor Tamura joined the Ministry of Home Affairs (currently the Ministry of Public Management, Home Affairs, Posts and Telecommunications). He had taught at the University of Tokyo's Graduate School of Arts and Sciences and the Local Autonomy College of the Ministry of Public Management, Home Affairs, Posts and Telecommunications before assuming his current position in 2002. His recent publications include "Daigaku ni okeru seisaku kenkyū kankei gakubutō no dōkō to chihōbunken jidai ni okeru jinzai ikusei" (The trend of founding policy research departments in universities and the nurturing of talented people in the age of decentralization) in *Jichi kenkyū* (Autonomy research, 2001) and "Eikoku no chihō jichitai ni okeru chīfu eguzekutibu no yakuwari" (The role of chief executives in U.K. local governments) in *Kōmu kenkyū* (Public service research, 2000).

# Index

administrative reform, 24–27, 36–38
agency-delegated function (ADF), 15, 22, 32–34, 36, 171
aging society, 26, 104, 140, 162
costs of, 137
Alien Registration Law, 65
Arete Childcare Services, 52–53, 60n. 3

Brazilians of Japanese descent, 64, 68–69, 79, 81, 85n. 10, 99, 102
Brookings Institution, 113–114, 116
*buraku,* 73
bureaucracy, central, 111, 162
and decentralization, 28, 36, 146
and LDP, 26–27
reform of, 28, 36, 38

centralization, 27
central government, 111
and international activities, 103
and local governments, 22–24, 41, 171
revenue to, 134–135, 137–148, 156–157
and NPOs, 173–176
and recession, 139, 141, 143
reorganization of, 31, 35–38
and resident foreigners, 64
education for, 70–71

policy toward, 65, 69–82
social security for, 70
and taxes, 138–139, 153 (*see also* Local Allocation Tax)
central-local government relations, 23–26, 28–29, 31, 34–36, 41
and politics, 35
China
sister affiliations with, 93, 97, 102, 107n. 14
Chinese residents, 64, 68, 74, 79, 106n. 6
status of, 99
citizens, role of, 155–156
Committee for the Promotion of Decentralization (CPD), 28, 30–34, 39, 41, 144 147
and intergovernmental fiscal reform, 41–42
community business, 48–60
in Hyogo prefecture, 55–57
in the United Kingdom, 48–49
consumption tax, 150
corporate tax, 134, 138–139, 141, 150, 158n. 2
Council on Economic and Fiscal Policy, 144, 146–148
Council of Local Authorities for International Relations (CLAIR), 67, 81, 94, 106n. 2, 107nn. 13, 14

# Japan Center for International Exchange

Founded in 1970, the Japan Center for International Exchange (JCIE) is an independent, nonprofit, and nonpartisan organization dedicated to strengthening Japan's role in international affairs. JCIE believes that Japan faces a major challenge in augmenting its positive contributions to the international community, in keeping with its position as one of the world's largest industrial democracies. Operating in a country where policymaking has traditionally been dominated by the government bureaucracy, JCIE has played an important role in broadening debate on Japan's international responsibilities by conducting international and cross-sectional programs of exchange, research, and discussion.

JCIE creates opportunities for informed policy discussions; it does not take policy positions. JCIE programs are carried out with the collaboration and cosponsorship of many organizations. The contacts developed through these working relationships are crucial to JCIE's efforts to increase the number of Japanese from the private sector engaged in meaningful policy research and dialogue with overseas counterparts. JCIE receives no government subsidies; rather, funding comes from private foundation grants, corporate contributions, and contracts.

# Other JCIE Books

JAPAN

*Governance for a New Century: Japanese Challenges, American Experience*, edited by Thomas E. Mann and Sasaki Takeshi

*New Perspectives on U.S.-Japan Relations*, edited by Gerald L. Curtis

*Policymaking in Japan: Defining the Role of Politicians*, edited by Gerald L. Curtis

ASIA PACIFIC

*Asia Pacific Security Outlook 2003*, edited by Charles E. Morrison

*Asia Pacific Security Outlook 1997–2001*, edited by Richard W. Baker, Christopher A. McNally, and Charles E. Morrison (CD-ROM)

*China-Japan-U.S.: Managing the Trilateral Relationship*, by Morton I. Abramowitz, Funabashi Yōichi, and Wang Jisi

*China-Japan-U.S. Relations: Meeting New Challenges*, by Morton I. Abramowitz, Funabashi Yōichi, and Wang Jisi

*Coping with 9-11: Asian Perspectives on Global and Regional Order*, edited by Han Sung-Joo

*Engaging Russia in Asia Pacific*, edited by Watanabe Kōji

*Major Power Relations in Northeast Asia: Win-Win or Zero-Sum Game*, edited by David M. Lampton

*New Dimensions of China-Japan-U.S. Relations*, edited by Japan Center for International Exchange

*Pacific Asia 2022: Sketching Futures of a Region*, edited by Simon S. C. Tay

*Rethinking Energy Security in East Asia*, edited by Paul B. Stares

*Road to ASEAN-10: Japanese Perspectives on Economic Integration*, edited by Sekiguchi Sueo and Noda Makito

## GLOBALIZATION, GOVERNANCE, AND CIVIL SOCIETY

*Changing Values in Asia: Their Impact on Governance and Development*, edited by Han Sung-Joo

*Deciding the Public Good: Governance and Civil Society in Japan*, edited by Yamamoto Tadashi

*Domestic Adjustments to Globalization*, edited by Charles E. Morrison and Hadi Soesastro

*Governance and Civil Society in a Global Age*, edited by Yamamoto Tadashi and Kim Gould Ashizawa

*Guidance for Governance: Comparing Alternative Sources of Public Policy Advice*, edited by R. Kent Weaver and Paul B. Stares

*The Third Force: The Rise of Transnational Society*, edited by Ann M. Florini

## HUMAN SECURITY

*Containing Conflict: Cases in Preventive Diplomacy*, edited by Satō Hideo

*Humanitarian Intervention: The Evolving Asian Debate*, edited by Watanabe Kōji

*The New Security Agenda: A Global Survey*, edited by Paul B. Stares

Japan Center for International Exchange
Fax: 81-3-3443-7580    E-mail: books@jcie.or.jp
URL: http://www.jcie.or.jp